SpringerBriefs in Economics

More information about this series at http://www.springer.com/series/8876

Dan S. Felsenthal · Hannu Nurmi

Monotonicity Failures Afflicting Procedures for Electing a Single Candidate

Springer

Dan S. Felsenthal
School of Political Sciences
University of Haifa
Haifa
Israel

Hannu Nurmi
Department of Political Science
University of Turku
Turku
Finland

ISSN 2191-5504 ISSN 2191-5512 (electronic)
SpringerBriefs in Economics
ISBN 978-3-319-51060-6 ISBN 978-3-319-51061-3 (eBook)
DOI 10.1007/978-3-319-51061-3

Library of Congress Control Number: 2016963359

Printed on acid-free paper

This Springer imprint is published by Springer Nature
The registered company is Springer International Publishing AG
The registered company address is: Gewerbestrasse 11, 6330 Cham, Switzerland

Contents

Chapter 1
Non-monotonic Voting Methods: An Overview

Abstract Voting is a necessary ingredient of democratic governance. Yet, there are numerous voting rules that differ from each other in processing the ballots into voting results. This is illustrated by examining a setting where five well-known rules each lead to a different election winner when operating on a fixed distribution of voter opinions. This observation has led to the study of voting procedures in terms of various desiderata. Our focus is on a specific set of desiderata that stem from the notion of monotonicity which characterizes those systems where any winning alternative remains a winner when its support is enlarged, *ceteris paribus*. This definition pertains to fixed electorates where the only possible changes involve improving the standing of the winning alternative with respect to some others barring all other types of changes. This concept should be kept distinct from Maskin monotonicity which maintains that whenever a winner improves its position with respect to some other alternatives and maintains its position *vis-á-vis* the remaining ones, it should remain the winner. These monotonicity concepts are defined for fixed electorates. There are other monotonicity-related properties definable in variable electorates. The best-known is undoubtedly the invulnerability to the no-show paradox. The paradox occurs whenever a group of voters obtains a better outcome by not voting at all than by voting according to its preferences, *ceteris paribus*. Of particular interest from the view-point of democratic governance are two extreme cases of the no-show paradox: the P-TOP and P-BOT ones. These will be focused upon in this book.

Keywords Monotonicity · Maskin monotonicity · No-show paradox · P-TOP paradox · P-BOT paradox · Democratic governance

1.1 Introduction

The latter part of the 20th and the first years of the 21st century have witnessed the victory of democratic ideals over their totalitarian counterparts at least on the level of political discourse, i.e., political programs, manifestos, debates and

D.S. Felsenthal and H. Nurmi, *Monotonicity Failures Afflicting Procedures for Electing a Single Candidate*, SpringerBriefs in Economics,
DOI 10.1007/978-3-319-51061-3_1

argumentation. Even systems that are based on blatantly non-democratic principles of governance invariably use popular will or the welfare of the people as the constitutional foundation of their existence. All modern systems seem to be based on the principle of government by consent. This idea in itself does not imply that the actual governing involves popular participation, but the latter is certainly compatible with it. Indeed, the consent is usually of repetitive nature and takes the form of elections for legislative and (in many systems) also for executive branches of government.

In providing an avenue for expressing the views of the electorate, the elections can be seen as fundamental mechanisms for providing legitimacy for the rulers occupying the positions of power as a result of the elections. *Going to the people* and *vox populi, vox Dei* are principles that capture the idea of elections as the final arbiter of political issues. Of course, it is inconceivable that all—or even most—political decisions would be made through elections. Modern governments are invariably of representative nature: people elect representatives and the latter make the collectively binding decisions in the name of the people. Thus, elections are undoubtedly a necessary—although not in itself sufficient—ingredient of democratic rule.

Both the people and their representatives engage in essentially similar activity, namely choosing the best alternative(s) out of a set of available ones. A wide variety of procedures have been invented for determining the choice. Part of the variety is due to the differences in the desired outcomes in terms of how many alternatives are to be chosen (e.g., choosing the president or choosing the parliament), what kind of input is expected from the voters (e.g., preference orderings over the entire set of alternatives or the set of best regarded alternatives), how the chosen alternatives are ordered (rank order over the chosen alternatives or just an unordered list of chosen alternatives), but even within each category of choice situations there are many procedures being used for the seemingly identical purpose, i.e., to elect the winner(s).

In this treatise the primary focus is on procedures used in single-winner elections, i.e., situations where the voters have to choose a single alternative or candidate as the winner. We start from the assumption that the voters have preferences about the alternatives at hand. These preferences may be widely different or relatively similar; we make no assumptions about the distribution of preferences among the voters. We shall investigate procedures or rules dictating the choice of winners, given the individual preferences about these alternatives.

It is well-known that different procedures may result in different winners even though no changes are made in the preferences of the voters (see e.g., Riker 1982, Nurmi 1987). In other words, the procedures are important determinants of the election results. To illustrate this, we use the following example that involves the preference orderings of 100 voters among five alternatives (*a–e)* under five well-known voting procedures (Nurmi 2004, p. 26).

No. of voters	Preference orderings[a]
45	$a \succ b \succ c \succ d \succ e$
22	$d \succ c \succ b \succ e \succ a$
33	$e \succ d \succ b \succ c \succ a$

[a]When the notation $a \succ b$ is used with respect to a single voter or with respect to a group of voters it means that the voter(s) rank(s) candidate a ahead of candidate b. When it is used with respect to the entire electorate it means that a majority of the voters rank a ahead of b

Consider the five voting procedures Plurality Voting, Plurality with Runoff, Copeland's rule, the Borda count, and Approval Voting. (The descriptions of these voting procedures appear in the next chapter in Sects. 2.4.1, 2.2.1, 2.3.4, 2.4.3 and 2.4.2, respectively). Given the above preference orderings among the five alternatives, we obtain that under Plurality Voting the winning alternative is a, under Plurality with Runoff the winning alternative is e, under Copeland's rule it is d, under the Borda count it is b, and under Approval Voting it is c (assuming that under this method the 45-member group approves of its top three alternatives while the remaining voters approve of their top two alternatives).

So which voting procedure should one, then, adopt? None of the above five procedures is downright irrational, undemocratic or unreasonable. They are all based on the information the voters provide about their preferences regarding the alternatives. However, this information is being utilized in the process of determining the winner in different ways by the different procedures. This in itself does not give an unambiguous answer to the question of which voting method one should adopt. Therefore we have to look at the properties of various voting procedures. More specifically, we should set up desiderata that a plausible voting rule should satisfy, evaluate the available procedures in terms of these desiderata and pick the best system accordingly.

If we had at our disposal a method for recognizing the right or correct decision, the problem of the best voting rule would be trivial: choose that rule which always ends up with the correct decision. But, alas, this kind of method is not available. Rather, the desiderata applied to voting rules pertain to the relationship between the expressed voter opinions and the outcomes ensuing from using a given voting rule for the set of voter preferences. The starting point in the analysis is the set of *individual preferences*, typically called a *preference profile*. The preferences of voters are assumed to be binary relations that are (i) *complete* (or connected) and (ii) *transitive*. By completeness we mean that for any two alternatives in the alternative set, x and y, either x is preferred to y, or y is preferred to x, or there is an indifference between x and y. Transitivity, in turn, means that for any triplet of alternatives x, y and z, the following holds: if x is preferred to y and if y is preferred to z, then x is also preferred to z.

We shall call a complete and transitive preference relation a *ranking*. If a preference relation is a ranking in this sense, the alternatives can be written in a *preference order*, i.e., a list where each alternative has one and only one position so that it is preferred to all alternatives on its right side (or below it, if the list is written vertically) and all alternatives on its left side (or above it) are preferred to it.

Most of the examples we use consist of profiles where the individual rankings are *anti-symmetrical.* This means that no voter is indifferent between any two alternatives or, in other words, the preferences of all voters are *strict.* The 100-voter example above is such a profile.

There is no shortage of voting system desiderata (see e.g., Felsenthal 2012; Richelson 1978; Straffin 1980). The best-known results in the theory of collective decision making pertain to the mutual compatibility or incompatibility of a set of voting system desiderata. One such result is *Arrow's impossibility theorem* which establishes an incompatibility of a relatively small set of desiderata (Arrow 1963; see also Kelly 1978).

Our focus in this treatise is on a relatively small but important subset of properties of voting procedures, namely the properties that relate to variations in the sets of winning alternatives under certain types of changes in voter preference orderings. The paradigmatic property in this subset is *monotonicity* which requires that winning alternatives remain winners when their support increases *ceteris paribus.* This intuitively natural requirement seems to underlie the very idea of going to the people. If this requirement is not satisfied, then it would seem that something else than the people is determining the social choice. Hence, procedures that are not monotonic can be viewed as suspicious from the democratic point of view. Indeed, we view monotonicity failures as the most serious pathology that may afflict voting procedures, so much so that procedures susceptible to monotonicity failures should perhaps be totally rejected as reasonable voting procedures.

Monotonicity is but an example of a wider class of properties that relate to intuitively plausible changes or lack of changes of social choices when the preferences of the electorate undergo certain types of changes.

1.2 Types of Monotonicity Failure

In mathematics the concept of monotonicity pertains to properties of functions. A function $f(x)$ of variable x is said to be monotonically increasing (or monotone increasing) if and only if an increase in the value of the argument x is associated with an increase in the value of $f(x)$. The function is monotonically non-decreasing if, whenever $y > x$, it follows that $f(y) \geq f(x)$. The concepts of monotonically decreasing and monotonically non-increasing functions are defined in an analogous manner. Since voting theory is basically a branch of social choice theory, one would expect that the concept of monotonicity of social functions would be similarly defined. The problem, however, is that social choice functions are not of one variable, but their arguments are preference profiles, i.e., n-tuples of preference rankings of the individual voters, assuming that they are n in number. Often an $n + 1$th argument is added, namely that denoting the alternative set, but this can be omitted if the alternative set under consideration is kept fixed or is otherwise known from the context. So, the social choice functions take the form:

$$F(A, R_1, \ldots, R_n) = \{x, y, z\}$$

where A is the alternative set, $R_1, \ldots, R_n$ the preference profile and $\{x, y, z\}$ is the set of winners chosen by F in this profile. The function is, thus, set-valued and its range consists of all subsets of A. Rather than set-valued functions one often speaks of social choice correspondences, i.e., multi-valued mappings. Either way, F specifies the winners once the alternatives and the preferences over them are given.

Now, how should one translate the concept of monotonicity to such correspondences or set-valued functions? The early solutions to this start from the notion of *positive association* and *responsiveness*. Thus, Arrow (1963, pp. 25–26) defines positive association of social welfare functions. These functions have the same domain as social choice functions, but their range is the set of all preference rankings over the alternatives. Accordingly, each profile is assigned a unique (collective) preference ranking. Suppose that in this environment there is a profile $R_1, \ldots, R_n$ over the set A of alternatives so that for a pair x, y of alternatives, the function ranks x higher than y, i.e., the former is collectively strictly preferred to the latter. Now suppose that we have a new preference profile $R'_1, \ldots, R'_n$ which is identical to the former profile except for the position of x: in the new profile x is at least as high in every individual's ranking in comparison to the original profile and possibly higher in some individual's ranking. The social welfare function is said to have the property of positive association if x is ranked higher than y also in the new profile. In other words, placing an alternative in a higher position, *ceteris paribus,* is never harmful to this alternative.

In his seminal work on the necessary and sufficient conditions for the simple majority rule in settings where only two alternatives are available, May (1952) points out that Arrow's positive association could also be called *positive monotonicity*. In his own analysis May focuses on mappings from the n-tuples of individual opinions regarding two alternatives, x and y, to collective opinions. Both individual and collective opinions can take on three values: either x is preferred to y, or there is an indifference between x and y, or y is preferred to x. May's positive responsiveness condition concerns situations where there is a tie between the two alternatives. It states that if, *ceteris paribus*, there is a change in the individual opinions that is favorable to one of the alternatives, say x, then x becomes the winner. In other words, only one change in the preferences is needed to break a tie and the ensuing outcome results in the alternative favored by the change. By a change that is favorable to x, we mean that an individual who prefers y to x, switches his/her preferences, or an individual who is indifferent between x and y, prefers x to y, or an individual who prefers y to x, is indifferent between the two.

In their definitions Arrow and May consider rules that differ from social choice correspondences. The former studies rules that transform individual preference profiles into collective preference rankings, whereas the latter focuses on methods of transforming individual three-valued decisions into collective ones.

For social choice functions, the relevant monotonicity concept is defined thus by Fishburn (1977, p. 476):

> A social choice function is monotonic if and only if alternative x belongs to the choice set in profile $R' = (A, R'_1, \ldots, R'_n)$ whenever x belongs to the choice set in profile $R = (A, R_1, \ldots, R_n)$ and R' is obtained from R by moving x up in one or several persons' preference orders without making any other changes, i.e., *ceteris paribus*.

This definition is obviously applicable to social choice correspondences as well since the range of social choice functions is assumed to consist of nonempty subsets of alternatives. Hence, they are point-to-set-mappings.

An important point to make here is that the groups of individuals in R and R' are the same, but the preferences of some individuals are different in the way indicated. The alternative set remains the same as well. Thus the only changes allowed for by the definition are associated with making a winning alternative more preferable in R' than in R for at least one individual. This can be expressed by requiring that the winner stays a winner whenever its support is increased, *ceteris paribus*. The importance of the *ceteris paribus* clause becomes evident once we proceed to another concept of monotonicity that is associated with the name of Maskin (1985).

What characterizes non-monotonic rules in Fishburn's definition is the possibility that added support, *ceteris paribus*, may turn winners into losers. Miller (2012) calls this possibility the *upward monotonicity failure*. Its mirror image is the *downward monotonicity failure*. This happens when an alternative that is a non-winner in a profile R, becomes a winner when some individuals rank it lower, *ceteris paribus*. In this case, then, diminishing the support, *ceteris paribus*, for a given alternative makes it victorious while it was not a winner when it had a larger support.

The monotonicity concept introduced by Maskin is defined as follows:

> Suppose that when using a given voting rule alternative x is chosen from the alternative set A when the profile is $R = (R_1, \ldots, R_n)$. Then another profile $S = (S_1, \ldots, S_n)$ over A is formed so that for any alternative y in A, the position of x with respect to y is at least as high in S as in R for all individuals. Then the *Maskin monotonicity* requires that x be selected in S as well.

It is to be noted that the electorates are of the same size in R and in S. The essential difference between Fishburn's and Maskin's monotonicity concepts is the absence of the *ceteris paribus* clause in the latter's monotonicity concept. It turns out that this makes Maskin's monotonicity a non-existent property among common voting rules. To see that the Plurality Runoff method is not Maskin-monotonic, let us look again at the above 100-voter example. As we stated, e is the winner under the Plurality Runoff method. Now, let us improve e's position in the rankings of all those 45 voters who rank it last so that e becomes now preferable to d by those voters. Since the *ceteris paribus* clause is not applied in Maskin's monotonicity concept we can freely move other alternatives *vis-à-vis* each other. So let us place b at the top of the rankings of the 45- and 22-voter groups. After these changes *b* clearly becomes the winner under the Plurality Runoff method. Thus, even though the previous winner *e*'s position has improved with respect to other alternatives, it is no longer the winner in the new profile. Hence, the Plurality Runoff system is not Maskin-monotonic.[1]

All the above monotonicity-related concepts deal with *fixed electorates* in the sense that the number of individuals remains the same and the focus is on what happens in collective outcomes when certain types of changes occur in individual preferences. Arguably, an equally important set of system properties pertains to situations where the electorate is *variable in size*. These properties are the central focus of the present work. More specifically, we will primarily be dealing with requirements imposed on rules regarding what happens in choice outcomes when the electorate is augmented with a group of individuals with certain kinds of preferences.

The first property in this set is analogous to the concept of monotonicity and is known as *invulnerability to the no-show paradox.* The most important thing that distinguishes this property from monotonicity is the electorate. In the no-show paradox the electorate is variable. The first article on the paradox written by Fishburn and Brams (1983, p. 207) contains the following definition:

No-show paradox: *the addition of identical ballots with x ranked last may change the winner from another candidate to x.*

Although clearly a surprising occurrence, this definition did not become standard in the voting theory, but had a second coming as the definition of *P-BOT paradox* discussed by Felsenthal and Tideman (2013) to which we will return shortly. Rather, the standard definition became the following one, also presented by Fishburn and Brams (1983, p. 212):

> … one of the candidates elected … could have ended a loser if additional people who ranked him in first place had actually voted.

Fishburn and Brams mention this paradox in the context of the single transferable vote system and attribute the finding to the *Report of the [British] Royal Commission Appointed to Enquire into Electoral Systems* issued in 1910. They also refer to Meredith's (1913) report. This older definition is now the standard one.

The invulnerability of a voting rule to the no-show paradox means that there are no profiles under which the rule would end up in an instance of the no-show paradox. Another way of saying this is that the rule satisfies the *participation axiom* (Moulin 1988). Thus, the participation condition and the invulnerability to the no-show paradox denote the same property.

[1] In contrast to Fishburn's monotonicity concept, Maskin's monotonicity concept does not seem to us compelling. It is therefore not surprising that not only the Plurality with Runoff procedure is not Maskin-monotonic, but that no other reasonable voting procedure is Maskin-monotonic.

Thus, we have defined the no-show paradox in terms of improvements of the outcomes from the view-point of a group of voters. The most dramatic instances of the paradox would be those where a group of identically-minded voters get their first-ranked alternative elected by not voting, while something less preferred by them is elected when they vote according to their preferences. Procedures allowing for this kind of possibility are violating the participation condition in a stronger sense and are vulnerable to the *strong no-show paradox* (Pérez 2001). In a slightly different terminology the procedures that are vulnerable to the strong no-show paradox violate the *positive involvement property* as defined by Saari (1995, p. 216). Richelson's (1978, p. 173) *voter adaptability condition* refers to the same property.

As we stated above, the definition that Fishburn and Brams (1983) gave for the no-show paradox was later on replaced by another one. Nevertheless, the paradox they referred to has not gone away nor has its importance been diminished thereby. What Fishburn and Brams called the no-show paradox is currently known as the *P-BOT paradox* (Felsenthal and Tideman 2013, pp. 70–71). The basic idea of the paradox is the following: if a candidate, say *c*, wins in a profile under some voting rule, then it may happen that another candidate, say *d*, wins if the original electorate is augmented with a group of like-minded voters who rank *d last* in their preferences. In other words, the added voters get their worst candidate elected when voting, but something more preferable to them wins if they abstain.

The most recent entrant in the set of participation-related properties is vulnerability to *double monotonicity failure* (Miller 2012). This failure characterizes a voting rule whenever there is a profile where *simultaneously* (1) additional support, *ceteris paribus,* renders the winner a non-winner, and (2) decreasing the support of a non-winning candidate, again *ceteris paribus*, would make him or her the winner. The double monotonicity failure—just as the monotonicity failure—is applicable to fixed electorates. Their counterparts in variable electorates have not yet been defined.

1.3 The Plan of the Book

This book deals with the monotonicity failures under both fixed and variable electorates. In other words, our focus is on counterintuitive changes in the voting outcomes when either some voters change their preference orderings or the electorates are changing as the result of new voters joining them.

Chapter 2 describes the 18 most well-known voting procedures for electing one out of several candidates. These procedures are divided into three groups: a group of five procedures that are vulnerable to non-monotonicity under both fixed and variable electorates, a group of eight procedures that are vulnerable to non-monotonicity under (only) variable electorates, and a group of five procedures that are invulnerable to any monotonicity failures.

Chapter 3 provides the theoretical background of the discussion on monotonicity-related failures and paradoxes of voting rules. Some basic theorems are presented and commented upon. The strategies of proof of these theorems are also presented.

Chapter 4 discusses and exemplifies the types of monotonicity failures of the five voting procedures which are susceptible to monotonicity failures under both fixed and variable electorates. Some insights into the types of environments where the failures and paradoxes occur will be given.

Chapter 5 discusses and exemplifies the types of monotonicity failures of the additional eight voting rules which are susceptible to these failures only under variable electorates. The variations of the no-show paradoxes under the various voting rules are the main focus.

The final Chapter 6 assesses the practical significance of the results and lists some open problems in the area of comparative analysis of voting rules.

References

Arrow, K. J. (1963). *Social choice and individual values* (2nd ed.). New York: Wiley.

Felsenthal, D. S. (2012). Review of paradoxes afflicting procedures for electing a single candidate. In D. S. Felsenthal & M. Machover (Eds.), *Electoral systems: paradoxes, assumptions, and procedures* (pp. 19–91). Berlin: Springer.

Felsenthal, D. S., & Tideman, N. (2013). Varieties of failure of monotonicity and participation under five voting methods. *Theory and Decision, 75,* 59–77.

Fishburn, P. C. (1977). Condorcet social choice functions. *SIAM Journal of Applied Mathematics, 33,* 469–489.

Fishburn, P. C., & Brams, S. J. (1983). Paradoxes of preferential voting. *Mathematics Magazine, 56,* 207–214.

Kelly, J. (1978). *Arrow impossibility theorems*. New York: Academic Press.

Maskin, E. (1985). The theory of implementation in Nash equilibrium. In L. Hurwicz, D. Schmeidler, & H. Sonnenschein (Eds.), *Social goals and social organization: essays in memory of Elisha Pazner* (pp. 173–203). Cambridge: Cambridge University Press.

May, K. O. (1952). A set of independent necessary and sufficient conditions for simple majority decision. *Econometrica, 20,* 680–684.

Meredith, J. C. (1913). *Proportional representation in Ireland.* Dublin: Ponsonby Ltd.

Miller, N. R. (2012). Monotonicity failure in IRV elections with three candidates. Paper presented at the Second World Congress of the Public Choice Societies, Miami, FL, March 8–11, 2012. Downloadable from http://userpages.umbc.edu/~nmiller/MF&IRV.pdf

Moulin, H. (1988). Condorcet's principle implies the no-show paradox. *Journal of Economic Theory, 45,* 53–64.

Nurmi, H. (1987). *Comparing voting systems*. Dordrecht: D. Reidel.

Nurmi, H. (2004). Monotonicity and its cognates in the theory of choice. *Public Choice, 121,* 25–49.

Pérez, J. (2001). The strong no show paradoxes are common flaw in Condorcet voting correspondences. *Social Choice and Welfare, 18,* 601–616.

Report of the royal commission appointed to enquire into electoral systems, HMSO, London 1910.

Richelson, J. T. (1978). A comparative analysis of social choice functions III. *Behavioral Science, 23,* 169–176.
Riker, W. H. (1982). *Liberalism against populism.* San Francisco: W. H. Freeman.
Saari, D. G. (1995). *Basic geometry of voting.* Berlin-Heidelberg: Springer-Verlag.
Straffin, P. D. (1980). *Topics in the theory of voting.* Boston: Birkhäuser.

Chapter 2
Descriptions of the Voting Methods to Be Analyzed

Abstract This chapter describes the 18 most well-known voting procedures for electing one out of several candidates. These procedures are divided into three groups:

- A group of five procedures that are vulnerable to non-monotonicity under both fixed and variable electorates: Plurality with Runoff, Alternative Vote, Coombs' Method, Dodgson's Method, Nanson's Method.
- A group of eight procedures that are vulnerable to non-monotonicity under (only) variable electorates: Successive Elimination, Bucklin's Method, Majority Judgment, Copeland's Method, Black's Method, Kemeny's Method, Schwartz's Method, Young's Method.
- A group of five procedures that are invulnerable to any monotonicity failures: Plurality Voting, Approval Voting, Borda's Count, Range Voting, the Minmax Method.

Keywords Voting procedures · Voting methods · Voting rules · Monotonicity failures · Fixed electorates · Variable electorates

2.1 Introduction

Felsenthal (2012) surveyed the susceptibility of 18 voting procedures discussed widely in the literature to various types of voting paradoxes. Only five of these 18 procedures were said to display simple monotonicity failure in fixed electorates: Plurality with Runoff, Successive Elimination, Alternative Vote, Coombs' Method, Dodgson's Method, and Nanson's Method. Thereafter Felsenthal and Tideman

This chapter is largely based on Felsenthal (2012).

D.S. Felsenthal and H. Nurmi, *Monotonicity Failures Afflicting Procedures for Electing a Single Candidate*, SpringerBriefs in Economics,
DOI 10.1007/978-3-319-51061-3_2

(2013, 2014) further analyzed the susceptibility of these five voting procedures to additional types of monotonicity failure under fixed as well as under variable electorates.

Of the remaining 13 voting procedures surveyed by Felsenthal (2012), Felsenthal and Nurmi (2016) showed that eight of them are susceptible to various types of monotonicity failure under variable electorates: Successive Elimination, Bucklin's Method, Majority Judgment, Black's Method, Copeland's Method, Kemeny's Method, Schwartz's Method, and Young's Method.

So of the 18 main voting procedures mentioned in the literature that are designed to elect a single candidate, five are susceptible to types of monotonicity failure under both fixed and variable electorates, eight are susceptible to types of monotonicity failure under (only) variable electorates, and only five methods are not susceptible to any type of monotonicity failure.

In the remainder of this chapter we shall first supply a brief description of each of the five voting procedures that are susceptible to some type of monotonicity failure under both fixed and variable electorates, then we will briefly describe the eight procedures that are susceptible to some type of monotonicity failure under variable electorates and, finally, we will briefly mention the most well-known five voting procedures that are not susceptible to any type of monotonicity failure and explain why this is so.

2.2 Five Voting Methods Susceptible to Types of Monotonicity Failure Under Both Fixed and Variable Electorates

2.2.1 Plurality with Runoff (P-R)

Under the usual version of this method, up to two voting rounds are conducted. In the first round each voter casts one vote for a single candidate. In order to win in the first round a candidate must usually obtain an absolute majority of the votes. If no candidate is declared the winner in the first round then a second round is conducted. In this round only the two candidates who obtained the highest number of votes in the first round participate, and the one who obtains the majority of votes wins. This is a very common method for electing a single candidate and is used, *inter alia*, for electing the President of France. For simplicity, P-R will be treated as operating on a single round of voters' responses, with the responses providing full rankings of the candidates, from which the voters' first choices from available candidates are taken. This simplification would affect the results only if voters using P-R wished to cast second-round ballots that were inconsistent with their votes in the first round.

2.2.2 *Alternative Vote (AV; aka Instant Runoff Voting; Ranked Choice Voting)*

This is the adaptation to the task of electing a single candidate of the multi-winner voting method known as the Single Transferable Vote (STV). STV was proposed independently by Carl George Andrae in Denmark in 1855 and by Thomas Hare in England in 1857. The use of this method for electing a single candidate was first proposed by an American, William Robert Ware, in 1871. It works as follows. All voters submit ballots that rank-order all of the candidates. In the first step one determines whether there exists a candidate who is ranked first by an absolute majority of the voters. If such a candidate exists s/he is declared the winner. If no such candidate exists then, in the second step, the candidate who is ranked first by the smallest number of voters is deleted from all ballots and thereafter one again determines whether there is now a candidate who is ranked first by an absolute majority of the voters. The elimination process continues in this way until a candidate who is ranked first by an absolute majority of the voters is found. The Alternative Vote is used in electing the president of the Republic of Ireland, the Australian House of Representatives, as well as the mayors in some municipal elections in the US. Beginning 2018 the state of Maine will be the first US state to elect by AV its governor, its Congressmen, as well as its state legislators. In May 2010 a referendum was conducted in the UK to decide whether AV should be used for electing the members of the House of Commons; a majority of voters rejected this proposal.

2.2.3 *The Coombs Method* (Cf. Coombs 1964, pp. 397–399; Straffin 1980; Coombs et al. 1984)

This method was proposed by the psychologist Clyde H. Coombs in 1964. It is similar to AV except that the candidate who is eliminated in a given round under the Coombs method is the candidate who is ranked last by the largest number of voters (instead of the candidate who is ranked first by the smallest number of voters as under the AV method).

2.2.4 *The Dodgson Method* (Cf. Black 1958, pp. 222–234; McLean and Urken 1995, pp. 288–297)

This method is named after the Rev. Charles Lutwidge Dodgson, aka Lewis Carroll, who referred to it implicitly in 1876 without explicitly endorsing it. It elects the

Condorcet winner when one exists.[1] If there is no Condorcet winner then the Dodgson method elects that candidate who can be made into a Condorcet winner by the smallest number of transpositions of adjacent candidates in the voters' rankings.

2.2.5 *The Nanson Method* (Cf. Nanson 1883; McLean and Urken 1995, Chap. 14)

The Nanson method is a recursive elimination method using the Borda method.[2] In the first step one calculates each candidate's Borda score. At the end of the first step the candidates whose Borda scores do not exceed the average Borda score of the candidates in this step are eliminated from all ballots and in the second step a revised Borda score is computed for each uneliminated candidate.[3] The elimination process is continued in this way until one candidate is left. If all of the uneliminated candidates have the same Borda score then one of them is elected according to a pre-determined method for breaking ties. If a Condorcet winner exists then the Nanson method elects him or her.

2.3 Eight Voting Methods Susceptible to Types of Monotonicity Failure Under Variable Electorates

2.3.1 *Successive Elimination* (Cf. Farquharson 1969)

This procedure is common in parliaments when voting on alternative versions of bills. According to this procedure, voting is conducted in a series of rounds. In each

[1]A Condorcet winner is a candidate who beats all other candidates in head-to-head contests. It is named after Marquis de Condorcet (1785) who proposed that if such a candidate exists s/he ought to be elected. When a Condorcet winner does not exist it is said that the majority method relation is intransitive and contains a top cycle, e.g., when there are three candidates the majority of voters rank candidate a above candidate b, the majority of voters rank candidate b above candidate c, but the majority of voters rank candidate c above candidate a. It is not entirely clear from Condorcet's book which candidate he thought should be elected when no Condorcet winner exists, although Peyton Young (1988) has made a highly plausible conjecture. (Cf. McLean and Urken 1995, Chap. 6). It should be noted that it is possible for a Condorcet winner to exist while the majority method relation among some or all of the remaining candidates is intransitive; it is also possible that neither a Condorcet winner nor a top cycle exist, e.g., when there are four voters—two with preference ordering $a \succ b \succ c$ and two with preference ordering $b \succ a \succ c$.

[2]For a description of the Borda score method see subsection 2.4.3 in the sequel.

[3]Many authors state erroneously that according to the Nanson method one eliminates at the end of each round only the candidate with the lowest Borda score, or only the candidates with below-average Borda scores, rather than all candidates whose Borda scores are equal to, or lower than, the average Borda score. Using the erroneous descriptions of the Nanson elimination process may result in different outcomes than those obtained under the correct Nanson elimination process.

round two alternatives compete; the one obtaining fewer votes is eliminated and the other competes in the next round against one of the alternatives that has not yet been eliminated. The alternative winning in the last round is the ultimate winner. If all voters vote in each round according to their true preference orderings among the alternatives then this procedure is Condorcet consistent.[4]

2.3.2 *Bucklin's Method* (Cf. Hoag and Hallett 1926, pp. 485–491; Tideman 2006, p. 203)

This voting system is named after James W. Bucklin of Grand Junction, Colorado, who first promoted it in 1909. In 1913, the US Congress prescribed (in the Federal Reserve Act of 1913, Section 4) that this method be used for electing district directors of each Federal Reserve Bank.

Under Bucklin's method voters rank-order the competing candidates. If there exists a candidate who is ranked first by an absolute majority of the voters s/he is elected. Otherwise for each candidate the number of voters who ranked this candidate in second place are added to the number of voters who ranked him/her first, and if now there exists a candidate supported by a majority of voters s/he is elected. If not, the counting process continues in this way by adding for each candidate his/her third, fourth, … rankings, until a candidate is found who is supported by an absolute majority of the voters. If two or more candidates are found to be supported by a majority of voters in the same counting round then the one supported by the largest majority is elected. However, it is unclear how a tie between two candidates, say a and b, ought to be broken under Bucklin's procedure when both a and b are supported in the same counting round by the same number of voters and this number constitutes a majority of the voters. If one tries to break the tie between a and b in such an eventuality by performing the next counting round in which all other candidates are also allowed to participate, then it is possible that the number of (cumulated) votes of another candidate, c, will exceed that of a and b.[5] So which candidate ought to be elected in this example under Bucklin's procedure? As far as

---

[4]A voting procedure is said to be 'Condorcet-consistent' if it elects a Condorcet winner when one exists.

[5]To see this, consider the following simple example. Suppose there are 18 voters who must elect one candidate under Bucklin's procedure and whose preference orderings among four candidates, a–d, are as follows: seven voters with preference ordering $a \succ b \succ c \succ d$, eight voters with preference ordering $b \succ a \succ c \succ d$, one voter with preference ordering $d \succ c \succ a \succ b$, and two voters with preference ordering $d \succ c \succ b \succ a$. None of the candidates constitutes the top preference of a majority of the voters. However, both a and b constitute the top or second preference of a majority of voters (15). If one tries to break the tie between a and b by performing the next (third) counting round in which c and d also are allowed to participate, then c will be elected (with 18 votes), but if only a and b are allowed to participate in this counting round then b will be elected (with 17 votes).

we know, Bucklin did not supply an answer to this question. This procedure is not Condorcet consistent (see Felsenthal 2012, p. 54).

2.3.3 *Majority Judgment* (Cf. Balinski and Laraki 2007a, b, 2010)

According to this proposed procedure, the suitability (or level of performance) of every candidate is assessed by every voter and is assigned an ordinal grade (chosen from a pre-specified range) reflecting the candidate's suitability or level of performance in the eyes of the voter. The candidate with the highest median grade is the winner.[6] In case of a tie between the median grades, denoted by α, of two or more leading candidates, one deletes one α grade from each of the tied candidates and then one computes for each of the tied candidates a new value of α, the median grade. If the new α grade of one of the (previously) tied candidates is higher than that of each of the other (previously) tied candidates, then this candidate is the winner. But if there is still a tie between two or more candidates with the new median grade α, then one deletes again one (new) α grade from each of the tied candidates, and the process continues until one finds a candidate whose α grade is higher than that of the others or, if no such candidate is found, one conducts a lottery between the candidates whose α grade is highest.

Although this is debatable, we assume that in single-winner political elections (as distinct, say, from sport competitions), a voter will award a higher grade to candidate x than to another candidate y if s/he prefers that x rather than y will be elected. If one accepts this assumption then the Majority Judgment (MJ) procedure is not Condorcet consistent (see Felsenthal and Machover 2008, p. 330; Felsenthal 2012, p. 59).

2.3.4 *Copeland's Method* (Copeland 1951)

According to this method one performs all paired comparisons. Every candidate x gets one point for every paired comparison with another candidate y in which an absolute majority of the voters prefer x to y, and half a point for every paired comparison in which the number of voters preferring x to y is equal to the number of voters preferring y to x. The candidate obtaining the largest sum of points is the winner.

---

[6] If the number of voters is even and a candidate's two middle grades are different, then the median is not uniquely defined. Balinski and Laraki take the lower of the two middle grades as the median grade. This asymmetry of the Majority Judgment procedure may create some problems as shown by Felsenthal and Machover (2008, Examples 3.2 and 3.7).

2.3.5 *Black's Method* (Black 1958, p. 66)

According to this (hybrid) method, one first performs all paired comparisons to verify whether a Condorcet winner exists. If such a winner exists, then s/he is elected. Otherwise the winner according to Borda's count is elected.

2.3.6 *Kemeny's Method* (Kemeny 1959; Kemeny and Snell 1960; Young and Levenglick 1978; Young 1988, 1995)

According to this method, too, one first performs all paired comparisons to verify whether a Condorcet winner exists. If such a winner exists, then s/he is elected. Otherwise Kemeny's method (aka the Kemeny-Young rule) specifies that up to $m!$ possible (transitive) social preference orderings should be examined (where m is the number of candidates) so as to determine which of these is the "most likely" true social preference ordering.[7] The selected "most likely" social preference ordering according to this method is the one for which the total number of votes with respect to pairs that are consistent with that ordering is maximized, and the candidate who ought to win is the one at the top of this ordering. Given the voters' various preference orderings, Kemeny's procedure can also be viewed as finding the most likely (or the best predictor, or the best compromise) true social preference ordering, called the *median preference ordering*, i.e., that social preference ordering, S, that minimizes the sum, over all voters i, of the number of pairs of candidates that are ranked oppositely by S and by the ith voter.[8]

---

[7]Tideman (2006, pp. 187–189) proposes two heuristic procedures that simplify the need to examine all $m!$ preference orderings.

[8]According to Kemeny (1959), the distance between two (individual) preference orderings, R and R', is the number of pairs of candidates (alternatives) on which they differ. For example, if $R = a \succ b \succ c \succ d$ and $R' = d \succ a \succ b \succ c$, then the distance between R and R' is 3, because they agree on three pairs [($a \succ b$), ($a \succ c$), ($b \succ c$)], but differ on the remaining three pairs, i.e., on the preference ordering between a and d, b and d, and between c and d. Similarly, if R'' is $c \succ d \succ a \succ b$, then the distance between R and R'' is 4 and the distance between R' and R'' is 3. According to Kemeny's procedure, the most likely social preference ordering is that R such that the sum of distances of the voters' preference orderings from R is minimized. Because this R has the properties of the median central tendency in statistics it is called the *median preference ordering*. The median preference ordering (but not the *mean preference ordering*, which is that R which minimizes the sum of the squared differences between R and the voters' preference orderings) will be identical to the possible (transitive) social preference ordering W which maximizes the sum of voters that agree with all paired comparisons implied by W.

2.3.7 *Schwartz's Method* (Schwartz 1972, 1986)

According to this method, too, one first performs all paired comparisons to verify whether a Condorcet winner exists. If such a winner exists, then s/he is elected. Otherwise Thomas Schwartz's method is based on the notion that a candidate x deserves to be listed ahead of another candidate y in the social preference ordering if and only if x beats or ties with some candidate that beats y, and x beats or ties with all candidates that y beats or ties with. The Schwartz set (from which the winner should be chosen) is the smallest set of candidates who are unbeatable by candidates outside the set. The Schwartz set is also called GOCHA (Generalized Optimal Choice Axiom). This method, too, is Condorcet consistent.

2.3.8 *Young's Method* (Young 1977)

According to this method, too, one first performs all paired comparisons to verify whether a Condorcet winner exists. If such a winner exists, then s/he is elected. Otherwise one elects that candidate who can become a Condorcet winner (or at least a majority non-loser) by removing the smallest number of voters from the electorate.

2.4 Five Main Procedures that Are not Susceptible to Any Monotonicity Failure

2.4.1 *Plurality (or First Past the Post) Voting Procedure*

This is the most common procedure for electing a single candidate, and is used, *inter alia*, for electing the members of the House of Commons in the UK and the members of the House of Representatives in the US. Under this procedure every voter casts one vote for a single candidate and the candidate obtaining the largest number of votes is elected.

This procedure is not vulnerable to any monotonicity failures for a simple reason: if a candidate, x, is elected by a given electorate—which implies that this candidate obtained the largest number of votes, then this candidate will surely be re-elected if, *ceteris paribus*, some of the original voters who originally did not vote for x will now change their minds and vote for x, or if, *ceteris paribus*, additional voters join the electorate and vote for x.

Similarly, if x was not originally a winner then the fact that, *ceteris paribus*, some voters lowered x in their preference orderings or that additional voters joined the electorate whose bottom preference is x cannot make x the winner because following this change x either loses votes or gains no new votes.

2.4.2 *Approval Voting* (Brams and Fishburn 1978, 1983)

Under this procedure every voter has a number of votes which is equal to the number of competing candidates, and every voter can cast one vote or no vote for every candidate. The candidate obtaining the largest number of votes is elected. So far this procedure has not been used in any public elections but is used by several professional associations and universities in electing their officers.

This procedure (which is but a special version of the Plurality procedure) is not vulnerable to any monotonicity failures for the same reasons that the Plurality procedure is not vulnerable to these failures.

2.4.3 *Borda's Count* (Cf. de Borda 1784; Black 1958; McLean and Urken 1995, pp. 83–89)

This voting procedure was proposed by Jean Charles de Borda in a paper he delivered in 1770 before the French Royal Academy of Sciences entitled 'Memorandum on election by ballot' ('Mémoire sur les elections au scrutin'). According to Borda's procedure each candidate, x, gets no points for each ballot in which s/he is ranked last, 1 point for each ballot in which s/he is ranked second-to-last, and so on, and $m - 1$ points for every ballot in which s/he is ranked first (where m is the number of candidates). The candidate with the largest number of points is elected. Thus if all n voters have strict preference orderings among the m candidates then the total number of points obtained by all the candidates is equal to the number of voters multiplied by the number of paired comparisons, i.e., to $nm(m - 1)/2$.

This procedure is not vulnerable to any monotonicity failures for a simple reason: if a candidate, x, is elected by a given electorate—which implies that this candidate obtained the largest number of points, then this candidate will surely be re-elected if, *ceteris paribus*, some of the voters who originally ranked x lower in their preference orderings will change their minds and rank x higher in their preference orderings, or if, *ceteris paribus*, additional voters join the electorate who will rank x at the top of their preference orderings.

Similarly, if x was not originally a winner then the fact that, *ceteris paribus*, some voters lowered x in their preference orderings or that additional voters joined the electorate whose bottom preference is x cannot increase the number of points obtained by x—thereby x must remain a non-winner.

2.4.4 *Range Voting* (Smith 2000)

According to this procedure the suitability (or level of performance) of every candidate is assessed by every voter and is assigned a cardinal grade (chosen from a pre-specified range) reflecting the candidate's suitability or level of performance in the eyes of the voter. The candidate with the highest average grade is the winner. This procedure is currently championed by Warren D. Smith (see http://rangevoting.org) and used to elect the winner in various sport competitions.

This procedure, too, is not vulnerable to any monotonicity failures. This is so because if a candidate, *x*, is elected by a given electorate—it implies that this candidate obtained the highest average grade. So this candidate will surely be re-elected if, *ceteris paribus*, some of the voters who originally awarded *x* a lower grade will change their minds and award *x* a higher grade, or if, *ceteris paribus*, additional voters join the electorate who will award *x* the highest grade.

Similarly, if *x* was not originally a winner then the fact that, *ceteris paribus*, some voters change their minds and now assign to *x* the lowest grade or that additional voters join the electorate who assign to *x* the lowest grade must decrease *x*'s average grade—thereby *x* must remain a non-winner.

2.4.5 *The Minmax Procedure*[9]

Although Condorcet specified that the Condorcet winner ought to be elected if one exists, Condorcet did not specify clearly, according to Black (1958, pp. 174–175, 187), which candidate ought to be elected when a Condorcet winner does not exist. Black (1958, p. 175) suggests that "It would be most in accordance with the spirit of Condorcet's … analysis … to discard all candidates except those with the minimum number of majorities against them and then to deem the largest size of minority to be a majority, and so on, until one candidate had only actual or deemed majorities against each of the others." In other words, the procedure attributed by Black to Condorcet when cycles exist in the social preference ordering is a Minmax procedure since it chooses that candidate whose worst loss in the paired comparisons is the least bad. Thus, for each candidate *x*, one first determines the maximum number of votes against him/her in any pairwise comparison. Let us denote this magnitude by $\mathrm{v}(x)$. The set of Minmax winners consists of those candidates whose $\mathrm{v}(x)$ value is smallest. When a Condorcet winner, say *z*, exists in a profile, it is clearly the only alternative in the set of Minmax winners since $\mathrm{v}(z) < n/2$, (i.e., the maximum number of votes any other candidate can muster against *z* is less than half the number of voters), while for every other candidate, *y*, $\mathrm{v}(y) > n/2$ (since each of them is defeated by *z*—and possibly also by some other candidate).

[9]Young (1977, p. 349) prefers to call this procedure 'The Minimax function'. It is also sometimes called in the literature 'the max-min method'.

The Minmax procedure is also known in the literature as the Simpson-Kramer rule (see Simpson 1969; Kramer 1977). This procedure is, of course, Condorcet consistent.

Although the Minmax procedure is the only procedure of those listed in Sect. 2.4 that is vulnerable to the related No-Show and Twin paradoxes (see Felsenthal 2012), it is invulnerable to any other form of monotonicity failure. This is so because if *x*, the candidate elected originally, is a Condorcet winner, then *x* remains a Condorcet winner under the Minmax procedure if, *ceteris paribus*, some of the voters who originally ranked *x* lower in their preference ordering will now change their minds and rank *x* higher in their preference ordering, or if, *ceteris paribus*, additional voters join the electorate who rank *x* at the top of their preference ordering. And if *x* was not originally a Condorcet winner then the fact that, *ceteris paribus*, some voters raised *x* in their preference orderings or that additional voters joined the electorate whose top preference is *x* must either cause *x* to become a Condorcet winner or further reduce *x*'s worst loss—thereby *x* must remain the Minmax winner. Similarly, if *x* was not originally a winner then the fact that, *ceteris paribus*, some voters lowered *x* in their preference orderings or that additional voters joined the electorate whose bottom preference is *x* must further increase *x*'s worst loss—thereby *x* must remain the Minmax non-winner.

In the next chapter we demonstrate the types of monotonicity failures that may be displayed by each of the five voting procedures listed in Sect. 2.2.

References

Balinski, M., & Laraki, R. (2007a). A theory of measuring, electing and ranking. *Proceedings of the National Academy of Sciences of the United States of America (PNAS), 104*, 8720–8725.

Balinski, M., & Laraki, R. (2007b). Election by majority judgement: Experimental evidence, (mimeograph). Paris: Ecole Polytechnique, Centre National De La Recherche Scientifique, Laboratoire D'Econometrie, Cahier No. 2007–28. Downloadable from https://hal.archives-ouvertes.fr/hal-00243076/document

Balinski, M., & Laraki, R. (2010). *Majority judgment: measuring, ranking, and electing*. Cambridge, MA: MIT Press.

Black, D. (1958). *The theory of committees and elections*. Cambridge: Cambridge University Press.

de Borda, J. -C. (1784 [1995]). Mémoire sur les élections au scrutin, *Histoire de l'academie royale des sciences année* 1781, pp. 651–665. Reprinted in I. McLean and A.B. Urken (1995), *Classics of social choice*, Ann Arbor, MI: University of Michigan Press, pp. 83–89.

Brams, S. J., & Fishburn, P. C. (1978). Approval voting. *American Political Science Review, 72*, 831–847.

Brams, S. J., & Fishburn, P. C. (1983). *Approval voting*. Boston: Birkhäuser.

Condorcet, M. (1785). *Essai sur l'application de l'analyse à la probabilité des decisions rendues à la pluralité des voix*. Paris: L'Imprimerie Royale.

Coombs, C. H. (1964). *A theory of data*. New York: Wiley.

Coombs, C. H., Cohen, J. L., & Chamberlin, J. R. (1984). An empirical study of some election systems. *American Psychologist, 39*, 140–157.

Copeland, A. H. (1951). A 'reasonable' social welfare function, *mimeographed*. University of Michigan, Department of Mathematics, Seminar on Applications of Mathematics to the Social Sciences.
Farquharson, R. (1969). *Theory of voting*. New Haven, CT: Yale University Press.
Felsenthal, D. S. (2012). Review of paradoxes afflicting procedures for electing a single candidate. In D. S. Felsenthal & M. Machover (Eds.), *Electoral systems: paradoxes, assumptions, and procedures* (pp. 19–91). Berlin: Springer.
Felsenthal, D. S., & Machover, M. (2008). The majority judgement voting procedure: A critical evaluation. *Homo Oeconomicus, 25,* 319–333.
Felsenthal, D. S., & Nurmi, H. (2016). Two types of participation failure under nine voting methods in variable electorates. *Public Choice, 168*(1), 115–135.
Felsenthal, D. S., & Tideman, N. (2013). Varieties of failure of monotonicity and participation under five voting methods. *Theory and Decision, 75,* 59–77.
Felsenthal, D. S., & Tideman, N. (2014). Interacting double monotonicity failure with direction of impact under five voting methods. *Mathematical Social Sciences, 67,* 57–66.
Hoag, C. G., & Hallett, G. H. (1926). *Proportional representation*. New York: The Macmillan Co.
Kemeny, J. G. (1959). Mathematics without numbers. *Daedalus, 88,* 577–591.
Kemeny, J., & Snell, I. (1960). *Mathematical models in the social sciences*. Boston: Ginn.
Kramer, G. H. (1977). A dynamical model of political equilibrium. *Journal of Economic Theory, 16,* 310–333.
McLean, I., & Urken, A. B. (Eds.). (1995). *Classics of social choice*. Ann Arbor: University of Michigan Press.
Nanson, E. J. (1883). Methods of election. *Transactions and Proceedings of the Royal Society of Victoria, 19,* 197–240.
Schwartz, T. (1972). Rationality and the myth of the maximum. *Noûs, 6,* 97–117.
Schwartz, T. (1986). *The logic of collective choice*. New York: Columbia University Press.
Simpson, P. B. (1969). On defining areas of voter choice: Professor Tullock on stable voting. *Quarterly Journal of Economics, 83,* 478–490.
Smith, W.D. (2000). *Range voting*. Downloadable from, http://www.math.temple.edu/~wds/homepage/rangevote.pdf
Straffin, P. D. (1980). *Topics in the theory of voting*. Boston: Birkhäuser.
Tideman, N. (2006). *Collective decisions and voting: the potential for public choice*. Aldershot, Hampshire, England: Ashgate Publishing Ltd.
Young, H. P. (1977). Extending Condorcet's rule. *Journal of Economic Theory, 16,* 335–353.
Young, H. P. (1988). Condorcet's theory of voting. *American Political Science Review, 82,* 1231–1244.
Young, P. (1995). Optimal voting rules. *Journal of Economic Perspectives, 9,* 51–63.
Young, H. P., & Levenglick, A. (1978). A consistent extension of Condorcet's election principle. *SIAM Journal of Applied Mathematics, 35,* 283–300.

Chapter 3
Some Theoretical Results on Monotonicity-Related Properties of Voting Rules

Abstract This chapter gives an overview of some of the most important theoretical results related to monotonicity properties of choice rules in fixed and variable electorates. The earliest one is Smith's theorem from early 1970s. It deals with runoff systems based on scoring functions. Fishburn's theorem, on the other hand, links non-monotonicity to positional dominance and pairwise majority rule by showing that a reasonable combination of these is incompatible with monotonicity. Another theorem by Fishburn is related to runoff systems where a winner may be found on a single round if its support is high enough. The theorem shows that also these systems are non-monotonic. Of results pertaining to variable electorates Moulin's theorem is well-known. It shows that with more than three alternatives and at least 25 voters, all Condorcet extension rules are vulnerable to the no-show paradox. Pérez strengthens this result by establishing the incompatibility of Condorcet consistency and invulnerability to the strong version of the no-show paradox for nearly all known Condorcet extensions. Saari's theorem establishes the extreme variation of electoral outcomes in subsets of alternatives in some profiles. He also shows that in those profiles a particularly dramatic version P-BOT paradox occurs. The Muller-Satterthwaite theorem shows that all positively non-imposed Maskin monotonic choice rules are dictatorial. We present these theorems and sketch the proofs of some of them. Some comments of their relevance in choice rule evaluation are also presented.

Keywords Condorcet extensions · Runoff systems · Scoring rules · No-show paradoxes · Monotonicity · Maskin monotonicity

3.1 Smith's (1973) Theorem

As a mathematical concept, monotonicity is of long standing, but in social choice theory it is of relatively recent origin. The first result cited here is due to Smith (1973). It establishes an incompatibility between a large class of voting procedures and a social choice desideratum when the electorate is of fixed size.

D.S. Felsenthal and H. Nurmi, *Monotonicity Failures Afflicting Procedures for Electing a Single Candidate*, SpringerBriefs in Economics,
DOI 10.1007/978-3-319-51061-3_3

Theorem (Smith 1973, p. 1036) *No point runoff system involving two or more stages and non-trivial point systems is monotonic. More specifically, if such a system determines first place first, then a change of votes in a candidate's favor can remove him from first place. If it determines last place first, such a change can put a candidate in last place who was not previously there.*

In other words, if the system first picks superior candidates for runoffs and then proceeds to form the collective ranking of the inferior positions, it is vulnerable to upward non-monotonicity in the sense that additional support for a winner, *ceteris paribus,* may turn him or her into a non-winner. If the system works by filling the last positions of the collective ranking first, then it may fall prey to a downward non-monotonicity whereby additional support for a candidate, *ceteris paribus,* may put him or her last in the collective ranking even though s/he was not there before the additional support was rendered.

A point voting system is one where each position in a voter's preference rankings is associated with a given number of points. To determine the collective ranking, the points given by each voter to an alternative are summed to form the score of that alternative. For example, in Plurality Voting each first rank awards one point and all the other positions award zero points to an alternative. A non-trivial system is one where there are at least two different point numbers (e.g., zero and one). Point runoff systems are characterized by a process of elimination rounds. Under the most familiar Plurality Runoff system (discussed in Sect. 2.2.1) there are basically at most two rounds. Under Nanson's rule, the number of rounds may be larger. In any event the crucial defining property of the point runoff systems is that the elimination of candidates be done using a monotonic point voting system. Under the Plurality Runoff method, the system used for elimination is Plurality Voting, while under Nanson's rule it is the Borda count. Both of these point systems are known to be monotonic in the sense that the number of points associated with the first position is at least as great as that associated with the second position, etc.

Smith proves his theorem by means of the following example for all point systems involving three candidates. He asserts that the extension of the example to more than three candidates presents no problem and is left to the reader. Smith's example involves 37 voters divided into three groups whose preference orderings among three candidates, *a*, *b*, and *c*, are as follows:

Group I	Group II	Group III
8 voters: $a \succ b \succ c$	3 voters: $c \succ b \succ a$	2 voters: $a \succ b \succ c$
8 voters: $c \succ a \succ b$	3 voters: $b \succ a \succ c$	1 voter: $a \succ c \succ b$
8 voters: $b \succ c \succ a$	3 voters: $a \succ c \succ b$	1 voter: $b \succ a \succ c$

Suppose that in the first round the point voting system used associates one point for each first rank, *t* points (with $0 \leq t \leq 1$) for each second rank and zero points for each last rank. The second round takes place between the two alternatives with the largest score in the first round. In the latter round, one point is awarded to each first rank and zero points to each second rank.

The above distribution of the 37 voters reveals that the social preference ordering of groups I and II is cyclical. In both of these groups each alternative is ranked first, second and third equally many times. Hence, no matter which value is given to t (in the interval indicated), the scores of alternatives in the 33-voter sub-profile are identical. So, the last four voters belonging to group III decide the collective ranking of the alternatives. Clearly a's point sum is largest, $3 + t$, followed by b with $1 + 2t$ points, while c gets only $1t$ points. So, a and b make it to the second round, where a wins with 22 points against b's 15.

Now, suppose that the three voters in group II with $c \succ b \succ a$ ranking reverse their preference between a and b in a's favor to $c \succ a \succ b$. Similarly assume that the three voters in group II with $b \succ a \succ c$ ranking put a ahead of b to end up with $a \succ b \succ c$ ranking. In other words, assume that these six voters change their preferences in winner a's favor. As a result the new point sums for a, b and c are: $17 + 12t$, $9 + 13t$ and $11 + 12t$, respectively. Hence, b is eliminated and a and c proceed to the second round, where c defeats a by 19 points to 18. Thus, additional support for a turned it from the winner into a non-winner. A heuristic explanation for this is that the voters who moved a up also moved b down, thus changing who got eliminated first in a way that was more to a's disadvantage than the few extra points s/he received were to his/her advantage.

A comment on the proof is in order, though. To wit, while it shows that all point voting systems consisting of two or more rounds that eliminate worst candidates on the basis of point sums only are non-monotonic, the same 37-voter and three-alternative profile cannot be used to prove that Nanson's rule is non-monotonic. The reason is that in this rule the eliminated alternatives are determined not only by the point sums, but also by the distribution of those sums. Hence, the Borda scores of a, b and c in Smith's above example are 40, 37 and 34, respectively. Since the average score is 37, both b and c are eliminated whereupon a wins. Switching the preferences in a's favor by six voters as described above, leads to a new distribution of Borda scores: 46, 31 and 34. Again a wins. Hence, the example does not work in proving that Nanson's rule is non-monotonic. It can be used to show that the *modified version* of the rule where the Borda scores are used to eliminate alternatives one by one is non-monotonic. But this version is not the one that Nanson advocated.

It turns out, however, that Nanson's (unmodified) rule is non-monotonic. Examples demonstrating this are presented in Sects. 4.6.1.1 and 4.6.1.2.

3.2 Fishburn's (1982) Theorems

Another important theorem on monotonicity of social choice functions is due to Fishburn (1982). Similar to Smith's theorem, Fishburn's theorem too pertains to fixed electorates.

Theorem (Fishburn 1982, pp. 123–124) *Consider a three-element set of alternatives {a, b, c} and a choice function f over this set that has the following property: if in any profile a positionally dominates c and b positionally dominates c and if a is majority preferred to b, then a is the sole winner in the profile. All social choice functions having this property are non-monotonic.*

Fishburn points out that the result is essentially due to Smith (1973). It seems to have a far wider coverage, though, and its proof is different. Before repeating it, the basic concepts appearing in the theorem have to be defined. First, an alternative x positionally dominates an alternative y in a profile, if x is ranked first by strictly more voters than y, if it is ranked first or second by strictly more voters than y, and so on until the penultimate rank. More precisely, let x_i (y_i, respectively) denote the number of voters assigning x (y) to i'th position in their preference ranking, and let k be the number of alternatives. Then x positionally dominates y, if $\sum_i x_i > \sum_i y_i$, for all $i = 1, 2, \ldots, k - 1$. Second, x is majority preferred to y if more individuals prefer x to y than y to x.

It should be pointed out that Fishburn's—as Smith's—theorem provides a sufficient condition for non-monotonicity. What this means is that whenever the conditions listed in the theorem hold, the system under investigation is non-monotonic. The theorem does not state that the conditions are necessary for non-monotonicity. It says nothing about systems that do not satisfy the conditions of the theorem.

Fishburn's proof uses the following example. Suppose there are 27 voters whose preference orderings among three candidates, *a*, *b*, and *c*, are as follows:

No. of voters	Preference orderings
6	$a \succ b \succ c$
3	$a \succ c \succ b$
4	$b \succ a \succ c$
6	$b \succ c \succ a$
6	$c \succ a \succ b$
2	$c \succ b \succ a$

From these voters' preference orderings one can see that *a* and *b* positionally dominate *c* and, moreover, *a* beats *b* in pairwise comparison. Hence, any rule satisfying the two properties has to end up with *a* as the winner.

Now suppose that, *ceteris paribus*, three of the four $b \succ a \succ c$ voters change their preference ordering in favor of *a* to $a \succ b \succ c$ and, similarly, the two $c \succ b \succ a$ voters also change their preference ordering in favor of *a* to $c \succ a \succ b$. As a result we get:

No. of voters	Preference orderings
9	$a \succ b \succ c$
3	$a \succ c \succ b$
1	$b \succ a \succ c$
6	$b \succ c \succ a$
8	$c \succ a \succ b$
0	$c \succ b \succ a$

Here *a* and *c* positionally dominate *b*. Furthermore, *c* is majority preferred to *a*. Hence the rule satisfying the above two properties should now choose *c*. These choices, however, prove that the choice rule is not monotonic since the second profile is obtained from the first one by improving the position of *a*, the winner in the first profile.

Looking at Fishburn's example from the angle of Nanson's rule reveals that this rule ends up with *a* in both profiles i.e., monotonicity is not violated in this profile when Nanson's rule is applied. If, on the other hand, Nanson's rule is modified so that at each stage of the elimination process only those alternatives that have the smallest Borda score are eliminated, then the *modified* Nanson's rule ends up with *a* in the first part of Fishburn's example and with *c* in the second part. In other words, this modification leads to the violation of monotonicity in Fishburn's example.

Besides Nanson's rule there is another non-monotonic system which does not satisfy the conditions of the theorem in Fishburn's example, namely Dodgson's rule introduced in Sect. 2.2.4. In Fishburn's example profile, it is *b* that in the first part of the example requires the smallest number of preference reversals to become the Condorcet winner. Hence the switch to the second part of the example is not one that would improve the winner's position, *ceteris paribus*. It turns out, however, that Dodgson's rule is non-monotonic. Fishburn (1977, pp. 472, 478) has shown this focusing on a somewhat modified version of the rule, but the same conclusion applies to the standard version as well (Nurmi 2004, p. 38). The non-monotonicity of Dodgson's method is exemplified in Sect. 4.5 (under fixed electorates) and in Sect. 4.9 (under variable electorates).

There are methods that look like point runoff systems, but on closer inspection are not. Nanson's rule is one of them, but more common ones are Alternative Vote and Plurality Runoff systems. What makes the latter two different from point runoff systems is that depending on the distribution of preferences there may not be a runoff contest at all. Instead, the winner is found on the first count. This is the case when one of the candidates is ranked first by more than 50% of the voters. Yet, Fishburn (1982, p. 125) shows that these systems are non-monotonic. As the preceding one, this result too applies to fixed electorates.

Theorem (Fishburn 1982, p. 125) *Let $d > 0$. Consider a set of three alternatives and a point runoff system that has the two properties of the preceding theorem modified so that whenever there is an alternative that is ranked first by more than*

100(d + 1/3)% of the voters, it is the unique winner. Any such system is non-monotonic.

Following is an example of the monotonicity violation of such a system, when $d = 1/12$.

Suppose there are 453 voters whose preference orderings among three candidates, a, b, and c, are as follows:

No. of voters	Preference orderings
100	$a \succ b \succ c$
51	$a \succ c \succ b$
52	$b \succ a \succ c$
100	$b \succ c \succ a$
100	$c \succ a \succ b$
50	$c \succ b \succ a$

Here a positionally dominates c, and b positionally dominates c. Moreover, a is majority preferred to b. Although b has the largest number of first ranks (152), it falls below the (5/12)% threshold of 453 which here amounts to 189 voters. Hence, the two properties dictate that a be chosen in this part of the example.

Now assume that, *ceteris paribus*, three of the 52 voters with preference ordering $b \succ a \succ c$ decide to increase their support of a by changing their preference ordering to $a \succ b \succ c$ and, similarly, two of the 50 $c \succ b \succ a$ voters decide to increase their support of a by changing their preference ordering to $c \succ a \succ b$. As a result we get:

No. of voters	Preference orderings
103	$a \succ b \succ c$
51	$a \succ c \succ b$
49	$b \succ a \succ c$
100	$b \succ c \succ a$
102	$c \succ a \succ b$
48	$c \succ b \succ a$

Here both a and c positionally dominate b. Moreover, c is majority preferred to a. Now a has the largest number of first ranks, 154. This is smaller than the 189 voter threshold. Hence the modified systems satisfying the two properties of Fishburn's first theorem elect c in the second part of this example. Thus, the improvement of a's position, *ceteris paribus*, turns it from being the winner to being a non-winner. Consequently the modified point runoff system too is non-monotonic.

One more important message from the preceding—and one that has been pointed out by Fishburn (1982, p. 133)—is that the number of alternatives under consideration plays a role in determining the monotonicity of procedures. There are rules that are monotonic when the number of alternatives is three, but become non-monotonic when larger alternative sets are being studied. This observation applies to other monotonicity-related properties as well.

3.3 Moulin's (1988) and Pérez's (2001) Theorems

The main results pertaining to the no-show paradox are due to Moulin (1988) and Pérez (2001). Before introducing them it is useful to discuss briefly a very popular social choice desideratum, namely the *Condorcet winner criterion*. It says that whenever there is a Condorcet winner in a profile, it should be the sole winner in that profile. It will be recalled that rules satisfying the Condorcet winner criterion are called *Condorcet extensions* or *Condorcet completions*. Sometimes—as in the following theorem—they are called *Condorcet consistent*. The criterion is central in the theorems of Moulin and Pérez. Can we say something about the relationship between the Condorcet winner criterion and monotonicity? Unfortunately not. There are Condorcet extensions that are monotonic under fixed electorates—e.g., the Successive Elimination procedure with a fixed agenda or Copeland's rule—and others that are non-monotonic—e.g., Nanson's and Dodgson's rules (see above and Fishburn 1982, p. 132).[1] This state of affairs is in stark contrast with the relationship between the Condorcet winner criterion and *vulnerability to the no-show paradox*. In the following theorem the phrase 'Participation' means invulnerability to the no-show paradox. The result pertains to variable electorates.

Theorem (Moulin 1988, p. 56) *If the set of alternatives contains no more than three alternatives, there are voting rules that satisfy Participation and Condorcet consistency. If the set of alternatives contains at least four alternatives and at least 25 voters, no voting rule satisfies Participation and Condorcet consistency.*

The first sentence is proven by showing that the Minmax rule is not vulnerable to no-show paradoxes when there are three alternatives. The proof of the second sentence proceeds via an auxiliary proposition stating that if b's margin of support against a, denoted by n_{ba}, is larger than the largest support margin that any alternative musters against b, denoted m_b, and if $|N| + m_b + 1 \leq |N_\infty|$, then a is not chosen by N. Here N refers to the original electorate and N_∞ is the set of potential voters. The auxiliary proposition is proven indirectly by showing that any Condorcet extension not satisfying this leads to a contradiction. So, all Condorcet extensions must conform to the auxiliary proposition. The proof of the theorem then

[1] As is shown in the second part of Chap. 4 and in Chap. 5, almost all known Condorcet-consistent rules are non-monotonic when the electorate is variable. The Minmax (Condorcet-consistent) rule is an exception: it is monotonic when the electorate is fixed and avoids both the P-TOP and P-BOT paradoxes (that are defined at the end of this section) when the electorate is variable.

proceeds by focusing on the following example depicting the preference orderings of 15 voters among four alternatives, *a*, *b*, *c*, and *d*.

No. voters	Ranking
3	$a \succ d \succ b \succ c$
3	$a \succ d \succ c \succ b$
4	$b \succ c \succ a \succ d$
5	$d \succ b \succ c \succ a$

Using the auxiliary proposition we find that: (1) *b* cannot be elected since $m_d = 5$, $n_{db} = 7$ and $|N| + m_d + 1 \leq 25$. In a similar way, it is shown that *c* and *d* cannot be chosen. Hence the choice must be *a*.

Now a set of four voters each with the preference ranking $c \succ a \succ b \succ d$ is added to get a 19-voter profile. Using again the auxiliary proposition it is found that *a* and *c* cannot be chosen in this profile. The outcome is then worse for the added four voters.

In a later study Pérez (1995) discussed several monotonicity-related properties of social choice functions when new voters are joining the electorate. Of more interest to the present work is, however, his article on the *strong no-show paradoxes* (Pérez 2001). From the view-point of the present treatise, the main results of this article can be summarized as follows. They pertain to variable electorates.

Result (Pérez 2001) *All commonly known Condorcet extensions are vulnerable to positive strong no-show paradoxes and failures of negative involvement, except for two extensions, namely the Minmax rule and Young's rule.*

The positive strong no-show paradox occurs when a group of voters with identical opinions on alternatives is not only better off by not voting than by voting according to their preferences, but the outcome resulting from their abstention is their first-ranked alternative. We are calling this paradox the *P-TOP paradox*. The failure of *negative involvement*, on the other hand, is what we are calling the *P-BOT paradox*: an alternative, say *x*, wins in a profile *P*, but when a voter whose bottom-ranked alternative is *y* joins *P*, *ceteris paribus*, *y* wins.

3.4 Saari's (1989) Results

Shortly after Moulin's (1988) article, Saari (1989) published a comprehensive study on the extreme procedure dependence of the voting outcomes under positional—and some binary—voting systems. This work uses a different methodology than the ones cited above and requires extensive introduction to be fully accessible. Hence, we restrict ourselves to only a couple of results that are most pertinent to our analysis. The first one relates to all plurality-based runoff systems, i.e., those that eliminate all but two best alternatives, those that eliminate all but three best alternatives, etc. The former part of the result deals with fixed and the latter with variable electorates.

Result (Saari 1989) *Consider* $k > 4$ *alternatives and suppose that in each subset the plurality rule is applied to form the collective ranking over the subset. There are (i)* $k - 2$ *runoff procedures, (ii) a profile of voters, and (iii) two added voters with identical ranking over the alternatives so that* x *is their top- and* y *their bottom-ranked, so that when the original voters apply i'th runoff procedure, the i'th alternative wins, for* $i = 1, \ldots, k - 2$. *Moreover, if the two added voters vote, the outcome remains the same in all elections except for the one where* x *(their top-ranked alternative) won. In this election their votes turn the outcome from* x *to* y *(their bottom-ranked alternative).*

This result is in fact a part of a corollary of a far more general theorem by Saari (1989, pp. 458–459). For our purposes it is particularly useful in covering all plurality-based runoff systems. The restriction to these systems turns out to be unnecessary as long as the procedure is *disjoint* (Saari 1989, p. 459) i.e., (1) selects the winning ranking in each subset of candidates with some positional system, (2) the final set of candidates is affected or determined by the subset rankings, (3) the final outcome (winner) is determined by the ranking over the final set of candidates (after eliminations) and (4) the method is not constant, i.e., at least two outcomes are possible. Saari shows that basically all disjoint systems are vulnerable to the no-show paradox.

3.5 Muller and Satterthwaite (1977) Theorem

Turning now to the *Maskin monotonicity* we again emphasize that it does not characterize any voting system we have dealt with in the preceding chapter. Apart from the path-breaking result showing that Maskin monotonicity is a necessary property of rules guaranteeing that the ensuing outcomes are *Nash equilibria* (Maskin and Sjöström 2002, p. 249), the best-known result on Maskin monotonicity (defined in fixed electorates) is due to Muller and Satterthwaite (1977). We adopt here the formulation of Aleskerov (1999, p. 212; 2002).

Theorem (Muller and Satterthwaite 1977) *Consider an alternative set of at least three elements and a single-valued choice function* F *that satisfies positive non-imposition and Maskin monotonicity. Then* F *is dictatorial.*

Positive non-imposition means that for any alternative x there is a profile so that F results in x. Since positive non-imposition seems eminently plausible, this theorem puts Maskin monotonic rules into the dubious group of dictatorial rules, i.e., rules where the social choice always coincides with the first-ranked alternative of a specific individual. In this view, the fact that no voting rule considered above is Maskin-monotonic is a virtue rather than vice. The proof is somewhat lengthy and proceeds via several lemmas. Hence it will be omitted here (but see, e.g., Aleskerov 1999, pp. 212–215).

The results discussed above are but a relatively small sample of those that pertain to monotonicity and related notions in the social choice theory. We believe, however, that we have included the most important ones. They—and occasionally some others—will be utilized in the following chapters.

References

Aleskerov, F. (1999). *Arrovian aggregation models.* Dordrecht: D. Reidel.

Aleskerov, F. (2002). Categories of Arrovian voting schemes. In K. J. Arrow, A. K. Sen, & K. Suzumura (Eds.), *Handbook of social choice and welfare* (Vol. 1, pp. 95–129). Amsterdam: Elsevier.

Fishburn, P. C. (1977). Condorcet social choice functions. *SIAM Journal of Applied Mathematics, 33,* 469–489.

Fishburn, P. C. (1982). Monotonicity paradoxes in the theory of elections. *Discrete Applied Mathematics, 4,* 119–134.

Maskin, E., & Sjöström, T. (2002). Implementation theory. In K. J. Arrow, A. K. Sen, & K. Suzumura (Eds.), *Handbook of social choice and welfare* (Vol. I, pp. 237–288). Amsterdam: Elsevier.

Moulin, H. (1988). Condorcet's principle implies the no-show paradox. *Journal of Economic Theory, 45,* 53–64.

Muller, E., & Satterthwaite, M. (1977). The equivalence of strong positive association and strategy-proofness. *Journal of Economic Theory, 14,* 412–418.

Nurmi, H. (2004). Monotonicity and its cognates in the theory of choice. *Public Choice, 121,* 25–49.

Pérez, J. (1995). Incidence of no show paradoxes in Condorcet choice functions. *Investigaciones Economicas, XIX(1),* 139–154.

Pérez, J. (2001). The strong no show paradoxes are common flaw in Condorcet voting correspondences. *Social Choice and Welfare, 18,* 601–616.

Saari, D. G. (1989). A dictionary of voting paradoxes. *Journal of Economic Theory, 48,* 443–475.

Smith, J. H. (1973). Aggregation of preferences with variable electorate. *Econometrica, 41*(6), 1027–1041.

Chapter 4
Five Voting Rules Susceptible to Types of Monotonicity Failure Under Both Fixed and Variable Electorates

Abstract In voting theory, monotonicity is the axiom that an improvement in the ranking of a candidate by voters cannot cause a candidate who would otherwise win to lose. The participation axiom states that the sincere report of a voter's preferences cannot cause an outcome that the voter regards as less attractive than the one that would result from the voter's non-participation. This chapter identifies three binary distinctions in the type of circumstances in which failures of monotonicity or participation can occur under five voting procedures (Plurality with Runoff, Alternative Vote, Dodgson's, Nanson's, and Coombs' methods) either when the electorate is of fixed or of variable size. The distinction that is unique to monotonicity is whether the voters whose changed rankings demonstrate non-monotonicity are better or worse off. The distinction that is unique to participation is whether the marginally participating voter causes his first choice to lose or his last choice to win. The overlapping distinction is whether the profile of voters' ranking has a Condorcet winner or a cycle at the top. The chapter traces the occurrence of all the resulting combinations of characteristics in the voting methods that can exhibit failures of monotonicity.

Keywords Elections · Non-monotonicity · Participation · Strategic voting · Voting paradoxes · Voting methods · Voting procedures

4.1 Introduction

In this chapter we shall demonstrate types of monotonicity failures under both fixed and variable electorates to which the five voting procedures described in Sect. 2.2 are susceptible.

Monotonicity failure under fixed electorates requires that some voters' reported rankings change as the example unfolds. We call these voters *dynamic* voters. Such changes in the rankings of voters might come from two different sources. First,

---

This chapter is largely based on Felsenthal and Tideman (2013, 2014).

D.S. Felsenthal and H. Nurmi, *Monotonicity Failures Afflicting Procedures for Electing a Single Candidate*, SpringerBriefs in Economics,
DOI 10.1007/978-3-319-51061-3_4

voters might change their true preferences as a result of additional information or as a result of campaigning by candidates and their supporters. Second, voters might decide to change their reported rankings strategically while their true preferences remained fixed. When a change in the reported rankings of dynamic voters causes a change in the winning candidate, the dynamic voters could be either better off or worse off. We say that an instance of monotonicity failure is of type [B] if the dynamic voters are better off and of type [W] if the dynamic voters are worse off. If the change is the result of strategic efforts, type [B] monotonicity failures represent successful strategic effort, while type [W] monotonicity failures would represent strategic efforts that backfired. If the change in reported rankings is the result of campaigning, then type [B] monotonicity failures represent situations in which the dynamic voters became even better off than they would have become if the candidate who rose in their rankings had won, while type [W] monotonicity failures represent situations in which the dynamic voters, both by their original ranking and by their revised rankings, become worse off than they would have been if they had reported unchanged rankings.

We employ the convention of assuming that the rankings first reported by the dynamic voters represent their true preferences, so that we can specify whether the change in their ranking makes them better off or worse off.

In addition to the distinction between type [B] and type [W] instances of monotonicity failures, there is a distinction between instances in which a winning candidate moves upward in the rankings of dynamic voters and thereby loses, and instances in which a losing candidate moves downward in the rankings of dynamic voters and thereby wins. We call the first type [U] and the second [D]. So starting from an initial situation [I] there can be up to four types of monotonicity failure that contribute to interacted monotonicity failure under each of the investigated voting methods, as follows:

1. [UB]: The winning candidate moves upward [U] in the rankings of the dynamic voters and thereby loses, and the dynamic voters are better-off [B] from changing their reported rankings, treating their original rankings as their true rankings.
2. [UW]: The winning candidate moves upward [U] in the rankings of the dynamic voters and thereby loses, and the dynamic voters are worse-off (W) from changing their rankings, treating their original rankings as their true rankings.
3. [DB]: A losing candidate moves downward [D] in the rankings of the dynamic voters and thereby wins, and the dynamic voters are better off [B], treating their original rankings as their true rankings.
4. [DW]: A losing candidate moves downward [D] in the rankings of the dynamic voters and thereby wins, and the dynamic voters are worse off [W], treating their original rankings as their true rankings.

Under fixed electorates we provide examples that show that for each of the five voting rules we investigate in this chapter, there is a *single* ballot profile containing either a Condorcet winner or a top cycle that is vulnerable to as many of the four sub-types ([UB], [UW], [DB] and [DW]) as are possible for that voting rule. In those cases in which it is impossible to demonstrate a failure, we explain why.

Monotonicity failures under variable electorates require an increase in the original electorate in order to demonstrate two possible paradoxes. The first paradox arises if one of the candidates, say candidate x, has been elected initially, then it is possible that another candidate, y, will be elected if, *ceteris paribus, the electorate is increased* as a result of additional voters whose *top-ranked* candidate is x join the electorate. The second paradox arises if one of the candidates, say candidate z, has not been elected initially, then it is possible that candidate z will be elected if, *ceteris paribus, the electorate is increased* as a result of additional voters whose *bottom-ranked* candidate is z join the electorate. We denote the first paradox as P-TOP and the second as P-BOT. Obviously the dynamic (added) voters are worse off under both paradoxes. So we only distinguish between initial situations where a Condorcet winner (CW) exists and situations where the social preference ordering includes a top cycle (CYC).

4.2 Types of Monotonicity Failure of the Plurality with Runoff Method Under Fixed Electorates

4.2.1 *An Initial Situation with a Condorcet Winner*[1]

Suppose there are 403 voters whose rankings of four candidates, a, b, c, and d, are as follows:

No. voters	Ranking
26	$a \succ b \succ c \succ d$
40	$a \succ c \succ b \succ d$
32	$a \succ d \succ b \succ c$
20	$b \succ c \succ a \succ d$
76	$b \succ d \succ a \succ c$
92	$c \succ a \succ d \succ b$
5	$c \succ b \succ a \succ d$
12	$c \succ d \succ a \succ b$
100	$d \succ a \succ c \succ b$

[1]Miller (2012) proved that double monotonicity failure in three-candidate elections under the Alternative Vote (and the Plurality with Runoff) procedure can occur only when a top cycle exists. Thus under the Plurality with Runoff (and the Alternative Vote) procedure a necessary condition for double monotonicity failure to occur when a Condorcet winner exists initially is that there be at least four candidates.

With these rankings, candidate a is the Condorcet winner. However, as no candidate is ranked first by an absolute majority of the voters, candidates a and b are both eliminated in the first round under P-R, and thereafter candidate d beats candidate c in the second round 208 to 195 and thus becomes the ultimate winner.

4.2.1.1 Upward Monotonicity Failure—Dynamic Voters Better Off [UB]

Now suppose that, *ceteris paribus*, 12 out of the 92 voters whose initial ranking is $c \succ a \succ d \succ b$ (who are not happy with the prospect that d will be elected if all voters rank the candidates sincerely), decide to change their ranking (strategically) to $d \succ c \succ a \succ b$ (thereby *increasing* d's support). As a result of this change b and c (rather than a and b) will be eliminated in the first round, and thereafter a will beat d 203 to 200 in the second round—thereby demonstrating the vulnerability of the Plurality with Runoff method to strategic upward monotonicity failure. Note that here the 12 dynamic voters benefit from strategically not representing their true preferences in their rankings.

4.2.1.2 Upward Monotonicity Failure—Dynamic Voters Worse Off [UW]

Suppose instead that, *ceteris paribus*, all the 12 voters whose initial ranking is $c \succ d \succ a \succ b$ decide to change their ranking (strategically) to $d \succ c \succ a \succ b$ (thereby *increasing* d's support). As a result of this change b and c (rather than a and b) will be eliminated in the first round and thereafter a will beat d 215 to 188 in the second round—thereby demonstrating again the vulnerability of Plurality with Runoff method to strategic upward monotonicity failure. However, note that here the 12 dynamic voters are worse off from strategically not representing their true preferences in their rankings.

4.2.1.3 Downward Monotonicity Failure—Dynamic Voters Better Off [DB]

Suppose instead that, *ceteris paribus*, the five voters whose initial ranking is $c \succ b \succ a \succ d$ decide to change their ranking (strategically) to $b \succ c \succ a \succ d$ (thereby *decreasing* c's support). As a result of this change a and d (rather than a and b) will be eliminated in the first round and thereafter c will beat b 244 to 159 in the second round—thereby demonstrating the vulnerability of Plurality with

Runoff method to strategic downward monotonicity failure. Note that here the five dynamic voters benefit from strategically not representing their true preferences in their rankings.

4.2.1.4 Impossibility: Downward Monotonicity Failure—Dynamic Voters Worse Off [DW]

It is impossible to demonstrate an example under the P-R method of downward monotonicity failure where the dynamic voters are worse off as a result of strategically not representing their true preferences in their rankings. To understand why this is so, let the initial winner be candidate *a* and let candidate *b* be the initial loser who is moved further down in some voters' rankings and as a result wins. For the dynamic voters to be worse off as a result of *b*'s winning they must initially rank *a* ahead of *b*. Under the Plurality with Runoff method, any change in rankings of the candidates below *a* is consequential only if and after *a* has been eliminated in the first counting round. But if *a* wins and thus is not eliminated in the initial situation, then *a* cannot be eliminated when the only changes are in rankings below *a* in some ballots.

4.2.2 *An Initial Situation with a Top Cycle*

Suppose there are 127 voters whose rankings of three candidates, *a*, *b*, and *c*, are as follows:

No. voters	Ranking
32	$a \succ b \succ c$
9	$a \succ c \succ b$
9	$b \succ a \succ c$
38	$b \succ c \succ a$
30	$c \succ a \succ b$
9	$c \succ b \succ a$

With these rankings, there is a cycle among the three candidates ($a \succ b \succ c \succ a$). As no candidate is ranked first by an absolute majority of the voters, candidate *c* is eliminated in the first round under P-R, and thereafter candidate *a* beats candidate *b* in the second round 71 to 56 and thus becomes the ultimate winner.

4.2.2.1 Upward Monotonicity Failure—Dynamic Voters Better Off [UB]

Now suppose that, *ceteris paribus*, nine out of the 38 voters whose initial ranking is $b \succ c \succ a$ (who are not happy with the prospect that a will be elected if all voters rank the candidates sincerely), decide to change their ranking (strategically) to $a \succ b \succ c$ (thereby *increasing* a's support). As a result of this change b (rather than c) will be eliminated in the first round, and thereafter c will beat a 68 to 59 in the second round—thereby demonstrating the vulnerability of Plurality with Runoff to strategic upward monotonicity failure with a top cycle. Note that here the nine dynamic voters benefit from strategically not representing their true preferences in their rankings.

4.2.2.2 Upward Monotonicity Failure—Dynamic Voters Worse Off [UW]

Suppose instead that, *ceteris paribus*, all of the nine voters whose initial ranking is $b \succ a \succ c$ decide to change their ranking (strategically) to $a \succ b \succ c$ (thereby *increasing* a's support). As a result of this change, again, b (rather than c) will be eliminated in the first round and thereafter c will beat a 77 to 50 in the second round—thereby demonstrating again the vulnerability of Plurality with Runoff to strategic upward monotonicity failure. However, note that here the nine dynamic voters are worse off from strategically not representing their true preferences in their rankings.

4.2.2.3 Downward Monotonicity Failure—Dynamic Voters Better Off [DB]

Suppose instead that, *ceteris paribus*, three of the 38 voters whose initial ranking is $b \succ c \succ a$ decide to change their ranking (strategically) to $c \succ a \succ b$ (thereby *decreasing* b's support). As a result of this change a (rather than c) will be eliminated in the first round and thereafter b will beat c 76 to 51 in the second round—thereby demonstrating the vulnerability of P-R to strategic downward monotonicity failure. Note that here the three dynamic voters benefit from strategically not representing their true preferences in their rankings.

4.3 Types of Monotonicity Failure of the Alternative Vote Method Under Fixed Electorates

4.3.1 Initial Situation with a Condorcet Winner

Suppose there are 205 voters whose rankings of four candidates, a, b, c, and d, are as follows:

No. voters	Ranking
20	$a \succ b \succ c \succ d$
20	$a \succ c \succ b \succ d$
16	$a \succ d \succ b \succ c$
10	$b \succ c \succ a \succ d$
38	$b \succ d \succ a \succ c$
50	$c \succ a \succ d \succ b$
51	$d \succ a \succ b \succ c$

With these rankings, candidate a is the Condorcet winner. However, as no candidate is ranked first by an absolute majority of the voters, candidate b is eliminated in the first counting round under the AV method, candidate a is eliminated in the second counting round, and thereafter candidate d will beat candidate c in the third round 105 to 100 and thus become the ultimate winner.

4.3.1.1 Upward Monotonicity Failure—Dynamic Voters Better Off [UB]

Now suppose that, *ceteris paribus*, three out of the 50 voters whose initial ranking is $c \succ a \succ d \succ b$ (who are not happy with the prospect that d will be elected if all voters rank the candidates sincerely), decide to change their ranking (strategically) to $d \succ c \succ a \succ b$ (thereby *increasing* d's support). As a result of this change c and b (rather than b and a) will be eliminated in the first and second rounds, respectively, and thereafter a will beat d 113 to 92 in the third round—thereby demonstrating the vulnerability of the Alternative Vote method to strategic upward monotonicity failure. Note that here the three dynamic voters benefit from strategically not representing their true preferences in their rankings.

4.3.1.2 Upward Monotonicity Failure—Dynamic Voters Worse Off [UW]

Suppose instead that, *ceteris paribus*, nine of the 16 voters whose initial ranking is $a \succ d \succ b \succ c$ decide to change their ranking (strategically) to $d \succ a \succ b \succ c$

(thereby *increasing* d's support). As a result of this change a and d (rather than b and a) will be eliminated in the first and second rounds, respectively, and thereafter b will beat c 135 to 70 in the third round—thereby demonstrating again the vulnerability of the Alternative Vote method to strategic upward monotonicity failure. However, note that here the nine dynamic voters are worse off from strategically not representing their true preferences in their rankings.

4.3.1.3 Downward Monotonicity Failure—Dynamic Voters Better Off [DB]

Suppose instead that, *ceteris paribus*, four of the 20 voters whose initial ranking is $a \succ b \succ c \succ d$ decide to change their ranking (strategically) to $b \succ a \succ d \succ c$ (thereby *decreasing* a's support). As a result of this change c and d (rather than b and a) will be eliminated in the first and second rounds, respectively, and thereafter a will beat b 153 to 52 in the third round—thereby demonstrating the vulnerability of the Alternative Vote method to strategic downward monotonicity failure. Note that here the four dynamic voters benefit from strategically not representing their true preferences in their rankings.

4.3.1.4 Impossibility: Downward Monotonicity Failure—Dynamic Voters Worse Off [DW]

For the same reason mentioned in Sect. 4.2.1.4 under the Plurality with Runoff method, it is also impossible to demonstrate an example under the Alternative Vote method of downward monotonicity failure where the dynamic voters are worse off as a result of strategically not representing their true preferences in their rankings.

4.3.2 An Initial Situation with a Top Cycle

When there are only three candidates the elimination process and final outcome under Plurality with Runoff and the Alternative Vote methods are the same. Hence the 3-candidate example in Sect. 4.2.2, presented to illustrate the vulnerability of the Plurality with Runoff method to monotonicity failure with a cycle at the top, also serves to illustrate the vulnerability of the Alternative Vote method to that failure.

4.4 Types of Monotonicity Failure of Coombs' Method Under Fixed Electorates

4.4.1 An Initial Situation with a Condorcet Winner

Suppose there are 220 voters whose rankings of four candidates, *a*, *b*, *c*, and *d*, are as follows:

No. voters	Ranking
52	$a \succ b \succ c \succ d$
2	$a \succ d \succ c \succ b$
2	$b \succ c \succ d \succ a$
50	$b \succ d \succ c \succ a$
28	$c \succ a \succ d \succ b$
2	$c \succ a \succ b \succ d$
3	$c \succ b \succ a \succ d$
22	$c \succ d \succ a \succ b$
52	$d \succ a \succ b \succ c$
3	$d \succ b \succ c \succ a$
4	$d \succ c \succ a \succ b$

With these rankings candidate *d* is the Condorcet winner, but under Coombs' method candidate *d* (who is ranked last by the largest number of voters) will be eliminated in the first round, candidate *c* will be eliminated in the second round, and thereafter candidate *a* will beat candidate *b* in the third round 162 to 58 and thus become the ultimate winner.

4.4.1.1 Upward Monotonicity Failure—Dynamic Voters Better Off [UB]

Suppose now that, *ceteris paribus*, six of the 50 voters whose initial ranking is $b \succ d \succ c \succ a$ (who are not happy with the prospect that *a* will be elected if all voters rank the candidates sincerely), decide to change their ranking (strategically) to $b \succ d \succ a \succ c$ (thereby *increasing* *a*'s support). As a result of this change *c* (rather than *d*) will be eliminated in the first round, *b* will be eliminated in the second round, and thereafter *d* will beat *a* 133 to 87 in the third round—thereby demonstrating the vulnerability of Coombs' method to strategic upward monotonicity failure. Note that here the six dynamic voters benefit from strategically not representing their true preferences in their rankings.

4.4.1.2 Downward Monotonicity Failure—Dynamic Voters Better Off [DB]

Suppose instead that, *ceteris paribus*, the three voters with ranking $c \succ b \succ a \succ d$ decide to change their ranking (strategically) to $b \succ a \succ d \succ c$ (thereby *decreasing* c's support). As a result of this change b (rather than d) will be eliminated in the first round, d will be eliminated in the second round, and thereafter c will beat a 111 to 109 in the third round—thereby demonstrating the vulnerability of Coombs' method to strategic downward monotonicity failure. Note that here the three dynamic voters benefit from strategically not representing their true preferences in their rankings.

4.4.1.3 Downward Monotonicity Failure—Dynamic Voters Worse Off [DW]

Suppose instead that, *ceteris paribus*, two out of the 52 $a \succ b \succ c \succ d$ voters decide to change their ranking (strategically) to $a \succ b \succ d \succ c$ (thereby *decreasing* c's support). As a result of this change b (rather than d) will be eliminated in the first round, d will be eliminated in the second round, and thereafter c will beat a 114 to 106 in the third round—thereby demonstrating again the vulnerability of Coombs' method to strategic downward monotonicity failure. Note that here the two dynamic voters are worse off from strategically not representing their true preferences in their rankings.

4.4.1.4 Impossibility: Upward Monotonicity Failure—Dynamic Voters Worse Off [UW]

It is impossible to demonstrate an example under the Coombs method of upward monotonicity failure where the dynamic voters are worse off as a result of strategically not representing their true preferences in their rankings. To understand why this is so let a be the candidate who wins initially and thereafter loses as a result of being ranked higher. Let candidate c be the new winner. For the dynamic voters to be worse off, c must initially be ranked by them lower than a. But the fact that a was ranked by them initially higher than c cannot be consequential until all candidates below a in their rankings, including c, have been eliminated. Therefore there cannot be a candidate below a in the rankings of the dynamic voters who wins.

4.4.2 *An Initial Situation with a Top Cycle*

Suppose there are 61 voters whose rankings of three candidates, *a*, *b*, and *c*, are as follows:

No. voters	Ranking
20	$a \succ b \succ c$
2	$b \succ a \succ c$
16	$b \succ c \succ a$
18	$c \succ a \succ b$
5	$c \succ b \succ a$

With these rankings, there is a cycle among the three candidates ($a \succ b \succ c \succ a$). As no candidate is ranked first by an absolute majority of the voters, candidate *c* is eliminated in the first round under the Coombs method, and thereafter candidate *a* beats candidate *b* in the second round 38 to 23 and thus becomes the ultimate winner.

4.4.2.1 Upward Monotonicity Failure—Dynamic Voters Better Off [UB]

Now suppose that, *ceteris paribus*, the five voters whose initial ranking is $c \succ b \succ a$ (who are not happy with the prospect that *a* will be elected if all voters rank the candidates sincerely), decide to change their ranking (strategically) to $c \succ a \succ b$ (thereby *increasing* *a*'s support). As a result of this change *b* (rather than *c*) will be eliminated in the first round, and thereafter *c* will beat *a* 39 to 22 in the second round—thereby demonstrating the vulnerability of the Coombs method to strategic upward monotonicity failure with a top cycle. Note that here the five dynamic voters benefit from strategically not representing their true preferences in their rankings.

4.4.2.2 Downward Monotonicity Failure—Dynamic Voters Better Off [DB]

Suppose instead that, *ceteris paribus*, the two voters whose initial ranking is $b \succ a \succ c$ decide to change their ranking (strategically) to $a \succ c \succ b$ (thereby *decreasing* *b*'s support). As a result of this change *a* (rather than *c*) will be eliminated in the first round and thereafter *b* will beat *c* 36 to 25 in the second round—thereby demonstrating the vulnerability of the Coombs method to strategic downward monotonicity failure with a cycle at the top. Note that here the two dynamic voters benefit from strategically not representing their true preferences in their rankings.

4.4.2.3 Downward Monotonicity Failure—Dynamic Voters Worse Off [DW]

Suppose instead that, *ceteris paribus*, two of the 20 voters whose initial ranking is $a \succ b \succ c$ decide to change their ranking (strategically) to $a \succ c \succ b$ (thereby *decreasing* b's support). As a result of this change a (rather than c) will be eliminated in the first round and thereafter b will beat c 36 to 25 in the second round—thereby demonstrating the vulnerability of the Coombs method to strategic downward monotonicity failure with a cycle at the top. However, note that here the two dynamic voters are worse off from strategically not representing their true preferences in their rankings.

4.5 Types of Monotonicity Failure of Dodgson's Method Under Fixed Electorates

Because Dodgson's method is Condorcet-consistent, a necessary condition for it to display any kind of monotonicity failure in fixed electorates is that the majority method relation contains a top cycle in the augmented electorate.

4.5.1 *Initial Situation*

Suppose there are 154 voters composed of 7 groups whose rankings of 10 candidates, *a–j*, are as follows:

Group No.	No. Voters	Ranking
1	10	$a \succ c \succ b \succ d \succ e \succ f \succ g \succ h \succ i \succ j$
2	43	$a \succ d \succ b \succ g \succ c \succ e \succ f \succ h \succ i \succ j$
3	10	$b \succ a \succ c \succ d \succ e \succ f \succ g \succ h \succ i \succ j$
4	4	$b \succ e \succ c \succ h \succ a \succ d \succ f \succ g \succ i \succ j$
5	38	$b \succ e \succ c \succ h \succ j \succ a \succ d \succ f \succ g \succ i$
6	10	$c \succ b \succ a \succ d \succ e \succ f \succ g \succ h \succ i \succ j$
7	39	$c \succ f \succ i \succ a \succ j \succ b \succ d \succ e \succ g \succ h$

Each number in the body of the *matrix of paired comparisons*, below, is the number of voters who rank the candidate listed at the left of the row ahead of the candidate listed at the top of the column. Thus, for example, the number 63 in row a and column c denotes that 63 of the 154 voters rank a ahead of c and therefore its complement number (91) is listed in row c and column a. So for candidate a to become a Condorcet winner she/he must be ranked ahead of each of the other candidates by at least a simple majority (78) of the voters. Since a is already ranked ahead of all other candidates except c, 15 voters (78–63) who rank c ahead of a would have to change their ranking and rank a ahead of c. To do so with a minimal number of rank inversions, the 10 voters in group 6 must change their ranking from $c \succ b \succ a \ldots$ to $a \succ c \succ b$ (a total of 20 inversions), the 4 voters in group 4 must change their ranking from $\ldots c \succ h \succ a \ldots$ to $\ldots a \succ c \succ h \ldots$ (a total of 8 inversions), and 1 voter in group 7 must change his/her ranking from $c \succ f \succ i \succ a \ldots$ to $a \succ c \succ f \succ i \ldots$ (a total of 3 inversions), so the minimal number of rank inversions needed for a to become the Condorcet winner is 31 (20 + 8 + 3).

	a	*b*	*c*	*d*	*e*	*f*	*g*	*h*	*i*	*j*
a	–	92	63	154	112	115	154	112	115	116
b	62	–	95	111	154	115	154	154	115	115
c	91	59	–	111	112	154	111	154	154	154
d	0	43	43	–	112	115	154	112	154	77
e	42	0	42	42	–	115	111	154	115	115
f	39	39	0	39	39	–	112	112	154	78
g	0	0	43	0	43	42	–	112	115	77
h	42	0	0	42	0	42	42	–	115	115
i	39	39	0	0	39	0	39	39	–	116
j	38	39	0	77	39	76	77	39	38	–

Since each of the candidates d–j has at least one zero in their row, requiring a minimum of 78 inversions to become a majority, whereas each of the candidates a, b, and c needs to beat just one other candidate (c, a, and b, respectively), against whom some votes have already been received, we only need to determine the minimal number of ranking inversions that are required in order for a, b, and c to become the Condorcet winner.

We have already calculated that for candidate a to beat candidate c at least 15 voters with a total of 31 rank inversions would be needed. A similar calculation shows that for candidate b to beat candidate a at least 16 voters (78–62) with a total of 32 rank inversions would be needed,[2] and for candidate c to beat candidate b at least 19 voters (78–59) with a total of 38 rank inversions would be needed.[3] Since candidate a needs the smallest number of rank inversions (31) to become the Condorcet winner, she/he is the winner in this example.

[2]At least 16 voters of group 2 must change their ranking from $a \succ d \succ b \ldots$ to $b \succ a \succ d \ldots$, i.e., a total of 32 rank inversions.

[3]At least 19 voters of group 5 must change their ranking from $b \succ e \succ c \ldots$ to $c \succ b \succ e \ldots$, i.e., a total of 38 rank inversions.

4.5.1.1 Upward Monotonicity Failure—Dynamic Voters Worse Off [UW]

Suppose now that, *ceteris paribus*, eight out of the 10 voters in group 3 decide to change their ranking (strategically) from $b \succ a \succ c$... to $a \succ b \succ c$... (thereby *increasing* a's support). As a result of this change one obtains that the 154 voters are now split into 8 groups as follows:

Group no.	No. voters	Ranking
1	8	$a \succ b \succ c \succ d \succ e \succ f \succ g \succ h \succ i \succ j$
2	10	$a \succ c \succ b \succ d \succ e \succ f \succ g \succ h \succ i \succ j$
3	43	$a \succ d \succ b \succ g \succ c \succ e \succ f \succ h \succ i \succ j$
4	2	$b \succ a \succ c \succ d \succ e \succ f \succ g \succ h \succ i \succ j$
5	4	$b \succ e \succ c \succ h \succ a \succ d \succ f \succ g \succ i \succ j$
6	38	$b \succ e \succ c \succ h \succ j \succ a \succ d \succ f \succ g \succ i$
7	10	$c \succ b \succ a \succ d \succ e \succ f \succ g \succ h \succ i \succ j$
8	39	$c \succ f \succ i \succ a \succ j \succ b \succ d \succ e \succ g \succ h$

and the (reduced) matrix of paired comparisons among candidates a, b, and c changes to:

	a	b	c
a	–	100	63
b	54	–	95
c	91	59	–

As before, a still needs at least 15 voters (78–63) with a minimum of 31 ranking inversions to beat c;[4] b needs at least 24 voters (78–54) with a minimum of 40 ranking inversions to beat a;[5] and c needs at least 19 voters (78–59) with a minimum of 30 ranking inversions to beat b.[6] So now c (who needs the smallest number

[4]To minimize the total number of rank inversions at least the four voters of group #5 must change their ranking from … $c \succ h \succ a$ … to … $a \succ c \succ h$…, (8 rank inversions); the 10 voters of group #7 must change their ranking from $c \succ b \succ a$… to $a \succ c \succ b$… (20 rank inversions); and one of the 38 voters in group #6 must change his or her ranking from ...$c \succ h \succ j \succ a$ …to …$a \succ c \succ h \succ j$… (3 inversions), i.e., a total of 31 rank inversions (8 + 20 + 3).

[5]To minimize the total number of rank inversions at least the eight voters of group #1 must change their ranking from $a \succ b$… to $b \succ a$ (8 rank inversions), and 16 of the 43 voters in group #3 must change their ranking from $a \succ d \succ b$… to $b \succ a \succ$ d… (32 rank inversions), i.e., a total of 40 rank inversions (8 + 32).

[6]To minimize the total number of rank inversions the eight voters of group #1 must change their ranking from $a \succ b \succ c$... to $a \succ c \succ b$… (8 rank inversions), and 11 of the 38 voters in group #6 must change their ranking from $b \succ e \succ c$… to $c \succ b \succ e$ (22 rank inversions), i.e., a total of 30 rank inversions (8 + 22).

of rank inversions) becomes the winner. However, note that the 8 dynamic voters (now group 1) are worse off as a result of upgrading (strategically) *a*'s ranking because *c* (the current winner) is ranked by them originally lower than *a*.

4.5.1.2 Downward Monotonicity Failure—Dynamic Voters Better Off [DB]

As candidate *b* was not elected in the initial situation (Sect. 4.5.1), suppose that two of the four voters in the (initial) group #4 change their ranking from $b \succ e \succ c\ldots$ to $e \succ c \succ b\ldots$ thereby *decreasing* *b*'s support. As a result of this change one obtains that the 154 voters are now split into 8 groups as follows:

Group no.	No. voters	Ranking
1	10	$a \succ c \succ b \succ d \succ e \succ f \succ g \succ h \succ i \succ j$
2	43	$a \succ d \succ b \succ g \succ c \succ e \succ f \succ h \succ i \succ j$
3	10	$b \succ a \succ c \succ d \succ e \succ f \succ g \succ h \succ i \succ j$
4	2	$b \succ e \succ c \succ h \succ a \succ d \succ f \succ g \succ i \succ j$
5	38	$b \succ e \succ c \succ h \succ j \succ a \succ d \succ f \succ g \succ i$
6	10	$c \succ b \succ a \succ d \succ e \succ f \succ g \succ h \succ i \succ j$
7	2	$e \succ c \succ b \succ h \succ a \succ d \succ f \succ g \succ i \succ j$
8	39	$c \succ f \succ i \succ a \succ j \succ b \succ d \succ e \succ g \succ h$

and the (reduced) matrix of paired comparisons among candidates *a*, *b*, and *c* changes to:

	a	*b*	*c*
a	–	92	63
b	62	–	93
c	91	61	–

To become a Condorcet winner, *a* now needs that at least 15 voters (78–63) change their rankings (with a total of 33 rank inversions)[7]; *b* now needs that at least 16 voters (78–62) change their rankings (with a total of 32 rank inversions),[8] and

[7]To minimize the total number of rank inversions the two voters of group #4 must change their ranking from $\ldots c \succ h \succ a \ldots$to $\ldots a \succ c \succ h$ (four inversions), the 10 voters of group #6 must change their ranking from $c \succ b \succ a\ldots$ to $a \succ c \succ b\ldots$ (20 inversions), and the three of the 38 voters of group #5 must change their ranking from $\ldots c \succ h \succ j \succ a\ldots$ to $\ldots a \succ c \succ h \succ j\ldots$ (nine inversions), i.e., a total 33 rank inversions (4 + 20 + 9).

[8]To minimize the total number of rank inversions at least 16 of the 43 voters in group #2 must change their ranking from $a \succ d \succ b\ldots$ to $b \succ a \succ d\ldots$, i.e., a total of 32 rank inversions.

c now needs that at least 17 voters (78–61) change their rankings (with a total of 34 rank inversions).[9] So now b (who needs the smallest number of rank inversions) becomes the winner. However, note that the two dynamic voters (now group #7) are better off as a result of downgrading (strategically) b's ranking because b (the current winner) is ranked by them originally higher than a.

4.5.1.3 Impossibility: Upward Monotonicity Failure—Dynamic Voters Better Off [UB]

This case cannot happen under Dodgson's method. If the dynamic voters are to be better off by upgrading the initial winner, the new winner must be a candidate that they rank above the initial winner. But the total number of rank inversions associated with the initial winner cannot increase if she/he is upgraded, and the total number of rank inversions associated with those initially above the initial winner in the rankings of the dynamic voters cannot fall, so the initial winner must remain, *a fortiori*, the winner if she/he is upgraded.

4.5.1.4 Impossibility: Downward Monotonicity Failure—Dynamic Voters Worse Off [DW]

This case, too, cannot happen under Dodgson's method. If one of the losers in the initial situation, say candidate b, is downgraded and as a result of this downgrading she/he were to win, the downgrading of b would need to harm the current winner. But the only possible harm is to candidates who are initially ranked below b and as a result of downgrading of b need additional rank inversions to get above those ahead of them. These are candidates that the dynamic voters find less attractive than b, so their worsened status must make the dynamic voters better off, not worse off.

4.6 Types of Monotonicity Failure of Nanson's Method Under Fixed Electorates

Similar to Dodgson's method, because Nanson's method too is Condorcet-consistent, a necessary condition for it to display any kind of monotonicity failure in fixed electorates is that the majority method relation contains a top cycle in the augmented electorate.

[9]To minimize the number of rank inversions at least 17 of the 43 voters in group #2 must change their ranking from … $b \succ g \succ c$ … to … $c \succ b \succ g$…, i.e., a total of 34 rank inversions.

4.6.1 Initial Situation

Suppose there are 16 voters whose rankings of six candidates, *a*–*f*, are as follows:

Voter no.	Ranking
1	$a \succ b \succ d \succ c \succ e \succ f$
2	$a \succ d \succ c \succ f \succ b \succ e$
3	$b \succ d \succ c \succ e \succ a \succ f$
4	$b \succ d \succ e \succ c \succ a \succ f$
5	$b \succ e \succ a \succ f \succ d \succ c$
6	$c \succ b \succ e \succ a \succ d \succ f$
7	$c \succ d \succ a \succ f \succ b \succ e$
8	$d \succ a \succ c \succ b \succ e \succ f$
9	$d \succ c \succ b \succ e \succ a \succ f$
10	$e \succ a \succ b \succ d \succ c \succ f$
11	$e \succ f \succ b \succ d \succ c \succ a$
12	$f \succ a \succ c \succ e \succ b \succ d$
13	$f \succ c \succ a \succ b \succ d \succ e$
14	$f \succ e \succ a \succ d \succ c \succ b$
15	$f \succ e \succ b \succ c \succ a \succ d$
16	$f \succ e \succ d \succ c \succ a \succ b$

In view of these rankings, the Borda score of each of the six candidates is equal to the sum of his/her respective row in the following matrix of paired comparisons:

	a	*b*	*c*	*d*	*e*	*f*	Sum
a	–	9	7	9	6	10	41
b	7	–	7	10	10	8	42
c	9	9	–	5	9	9	41
d	7	6	11	–	8	9	41
e	10	6	7	8	–	9	40
f	6	8	7	7	7	–	35
Total							240

The sum of the Borda scores of all six candidates is 240,[10] hence the average Borda score is 40 (240/6). According to the Nanson method, one eliminates at the end of every counting round those candidates whose Borda score does not exceed

[10]Note that the sum of all the voters' Borda scores can also be obtained by multiplying the number of voters (16 in this example) by the number of paired comparisons among all the candidates ($6 \cdot 5/2 = 15$ paired comparisons in this example).

the average Borda score of all the candidates participating in that round. So here candidates *e* and *f* are eliminated and a revised matrix of paired comparisons among the remaining four candidates is computed:

	a	*b*	*c*	*d*	Sum
a	–	9	7	9	25
b	7	–	7	10	24
c	9	9	–	5	23
d	7	6	11	–	24
Total					96

Here the average Borda score of the four voters *a*–*d* is 24 (96/4), so all candidates except *a* are eliminated and *a* becomes the winner.

4.6.1.1 Upward Monotonicity Failure—Dynamic Voters Better Off [UB]

Suppose now that, *ceteris paribus*, voter #7 (who would rather have *c* or *d* than *a*, who will be elected if all voters rank the candidates sincerely) decides to change (strategically) his/her ranking from $c \succ d \succ a\ldots$ to $c \succ a \succ d\ldots$ thereby *increasing a*'s support. So we now obtain the following matrix of paired comparisons and Borda scores:

	a	*b*	*c*	*d*	*e*	*f*	Sum
a	–	9	7	10	6	10	42
b	7	–	7	10	10	8	42
c	9	9	–	5	9	9	41
d	6	6	11	–	8	9	40
e	10	6	7	8	–	9	40
f	6	8	7	7	7	–	35
Total							240

As the average Borda score remains 40 (240/6), candidates *d*, *e*, and *f* are eliminated and a revised matrix of paired comparisons among the remaining three candidates is computed:

	a	*b*	*c*	Sum
a	–	9	7	16
b	7	–	7	14
c	9	9	–	18
Total				48

Here the average Borda score of the three candidates *a*–*c* is 16 (48/3), so all candidates except *c* are eliminated and *c* becomes the winner. Note that voter #7 benefited from (strategically) moving *a* up in his/her ranking because, *ceteris paribus*, she/he obtained as a result the election of *c* which she/he ranked initially above *a*.

4.6.1.2 Upward Monotonicity Failure—Dynamic Voters Worse Off [UW]

Suppose instead that, *ceteris paribus*, voter #8 decides to change his/her ranking from $d \succ a \succ c\ldots$ to $a \succ d \succ c\ldots$ thereby *increasing* *a*'s support. So we now obtain the same matrices and final results as in Sect. 4.6.1.1, i.e., here too candidate *c* is elected. The only difference is that here voter #8 is worse off as a result of (strategically) upgrading *a* because she/he obtains the election of *c* which she/he ranked originally lower than *a*.

4.6.1.3 Downward Monotonicity Failure—Dynamic Voters Better Off [DB]

As candidate *b* was not elected initially, suppose now that, *ceteris paribus*, voter #5 decides to downgrade candidate *b* by changing his/her rank order from $b \succ e \succ a\ldots$ to $e \succ b \succ a\ldots$. As a result, the initial Borda score of *b* decreases from 42 to 41 and the initial Borda score of *e* increases from 40 to 41, while the Borda scores of all the other candidates and the average Borda score (40) remain the same. So according to Nanson's method candidate *f* is eliminated after the first count, and we obtain the following (revised) matrix of paired comparisons and Borda scores of the remaining five candidates:

	a	*b*	*c*	*d*	*e*	Sum
a	–	9	7	9	6	31
b	7	–	7	10	9	33
c	9	9	–	5	9	32
d	7	6	11	–	8	32
e	10	7	7	8	–	32
Total						160

The (revised) average Borda score is now 32 (160/5), so all candidates except *b* are eliminated and *b* becomes the winner. Note that voter #5 is better off by downgrading (strategically) *b* in his/her original ranking, because as a result she/he obtains the election of *b* whom she/he prefers over the election of the original winner (*a*).

4.6.1.4 Downward Monotonicity Failure—Dynamic Voters Worse Off [DW]

As candidate *b* was not elected initially, suppose instead that, *ceteris paribus*, voter #2 changes his/her ranking from … $b \succ e$ to …$e \succ b$ thereby decreasing his/her support of *b*. So we now obtain the same matrices and final results as in Sect. 4.6.1.3, i.e., here too candidate *b* is elected. The only difference is that here voter #2 is worse off as a result of (strategically) downgrading *b* because she/he obtains the election of *b* which she/he ranked originally lower than *a*.

4.7 Types of Monotonicity Failure of the Plurality with Runoff and the Alternative Vote Methods Under Variable Electorates

4.7.1 Impossibility: P-TOP

Both the Plurality with Runoff and the Alternative Vote methods are not vulnerable to the P-TOP paradox. This is so because under these two methods, the candidate(s) who are top-ranked by the fewest number of voters are eliminated sequentially and the candidate who is top-ranked by an absolute majority of the voters is elected. Hence if *x* was elected initially under these methods then, *ceteris paribus*, *x* will be elected *a fortiori* if additional voters whose top-rank is *x* join the electorate. However, Fishburn and Brams (1983, pp. 211–213) demonstrate that the Single Transferable Vote method (of which the Alternative Vote method is but a special case) is vulnerable to the P-TOP paradox when more than one candidate must be elected.

4.7.2 P-BOT + CW

This example is due to Felsenthal and Maoz (1992, Example 5, p. 119). Suppose there are 19 voters whose rankings of three candidates, *a*, *b*, and *c*, are as follows:

No. voters	Ranking
4	$a \succ b \succ c$
1	$a \succ c \succ b$
2	$b \succ a \succ c$
4	$b \succ c \succ a$
3	$c \succ a \succ b$
5	$c \succ b \succ a$

The social preference ordering is $b \succ c \succ a$, i.e., b is a Condorcet winner. Under the Plurality with Runoff and Alternative Vote methods, candidate a is eliminated after the first round and b is elected in the second round.

As candidate c has not been elected, suppose now that, *ceteris paribus*, two additional voters whose ranking is $a \succ b \succ c$ join the electorate (thereby further downgrading c). As a result b is eliminated in the first round, and c is elected in the second round—thus demonstrating the susceptibility of the Plurality with Runoff and the Alternative Vote methods to the P-BOT paradox.

4.7.3 *P-BOT + CYC*

Suppose there are 102 voters whose rankings of three candidates, a, b, and c, are as follows:

No. voters	Ranking
20	$a \succ b \succ c$
13	$a \succ c \succ b$
13	$b \succ a \succ c$
21	$b \succ c \succ a$
35	$c \succ a \succ b$

The social preference ordering is cyclical ($a \succ b \succ c \succ a$). Under the Plurality with Runoff and Alternative Vote methods, candidate a is eliminated after the first round and b is elected in the second round.

As candidate c has not been elected, suppose now that, *ceteris paribus*, two additional voters whose ranking is $a \succ b \succ c$ join the electorate (thereby further downgrading c). As a result b is eliminated in the first round, and c is elected in the second round—thus demonstrating the susceptibility of the Plurality with Runoff and the Alternative Vote methods to the P-BOT paradox.

4.8 Types of Monotonicity Failure of Coombs' Method Under Variable Electorates

4.8.1 *P-TOP + CW*

Suppose there are 42 voters who must elect one of four candidates, a, b, c, or d, under Coombs' method, and that their rankings of the candidates are as follows:

No. voters	Ranking
7	$a \succ c \succ d \succ b$
6	$a \succ d \succ b \succ c$
3	$b \succ a \succ c \succ d$
7	$b \succ c \succ a \succ d$
9	$b \succ c \succ d \succ a$
4	$c \succ a \succ d \succ b$
6	$d \succ a \succ b \succ c$

Here a is the Condorcet winner. Since none of the candidates is ranked first by an absolute majority of the voters, candidate c is eliminated in the first round under the Coombs' method, candidate b is eliminated in the second round, and thereafter candidate a is elected.

Now suppose that, *ceteris paribus*, three additional voters join the electorate whose ranking is $a \succ c \succ b \succ d$. Although the number of voters who rank a first has now increased, still none of the candidates is ranked first by an absolute majority of the voters. So according to Coombs' method candidate d is eliminated in the first counting round, candidate a is eliminated in the second counting round, whereupon candidate b is elected thus demonstrating the susceptibility of Coombs' method to the P-TOP paradox.

4.8.2 P-TOP + CYC

Suppose there are 100 voters who must elect one of three candidates, a, b, *or* c, under Coombs' method, and that their rankings of the candidates are as follows:

No. voters	Ranking
40	$a \succ b \succ c$
15	$b \succ c \succ a$
30	$c \succ a \succ b$
15	$c \succ b \succ a$

Here the social preference ordering is cyclical ($a \succ b \succ c \succ a$). Since none of the candidates is ranked first by an absolute majority of the voters, candidate c is eliminated in the first round under the Coombs' method, and thereafter candidate a beats b and thereby becomes the ultimate winner.

Now suppose that, *ceteris paribus*, 11 additional voters join the electorate whose ranking is $a \succ c \succ b$. Although the number of voters who rank a first has now increased, still none of the candidates is ranked first by an absolute majority of the voters. So according to Coombs' method candidate b is eliminated whereupon candidate c is elected thus demonstrating the susceptibility of Coombs' method to the P-TOP paradox.

4.8.3 Impossibility: P-BOT

The Coombs method is invulnerable to the P-BOT paradox. This is so because under this method one eliminates sequentially the candidates who are ranked last by the largest number of voters. So if candidate z was not elected originally, then z can certainly not be elected under the Coombs' method if additional voters who rank z last join the electorate.

4.9 Types of Monotonicity Failure of Dodgson's Method Under Variable Electorates

4.9.1 Impossibility: P-TOP + CW

As Dodgson's method is Condorcet-consistent, it cannot display the P-TOP paradox when a Condorcet winner exists initially. This is so because if the Condorcet winner was elected initially then the Condorcet winner will be elected, *a fortiori*, when additional voters join the electorate whose top rank is the Condorcet winner.

4.9.2 P-TOP + CYC

This example is adapted from Fishburn (1977, p. 478). Suppose there are 100 voters who are divided into four groups, who must elect one of five candidates a, b, c, d, e under the Dodgson method, and whose rankings of the candidates are as follows:

Group	No. voters	Ranking
G1	42	$b \succ a \succ c \succ d \succ e$
G2	26	$a \succ e \succ c \succ b \succ d$
G3	21	$e \succ d \succ b \succ a \succ c$
G4	11	$e \succ a \succ b \succ d \succ c$

The majority relation method has a top cycle [($b \succ a \succ e \succ b$) $\succ c \succ d$]. It can be depicted in the following matrix of paired comparisons:

	a	*b*	*c*	*d*	*e*
a	–	37	100	79	68
b	63	–	74	79	42
c	0	26	–	68	42
d	21	21	32	–	42
e	32	58	58	58	–

So for candidate *a* to become a Condorcet winner she/he must be ranked ahead of each of the other candidates by at least a simple majority (51) of the voters. Since *a* is already ranked ahead of all other candidates except *b*, 14 voters (51–37) who rank *b* ahead of *a* would have to change their ranking and rank *a* ahead of *b*. To do so with a minimal number of rank inversions at least 14 voters who are either in group G1 or group G3 must invert $b \succ a$ in their rankings to $a \succ b$, i.e., a total of 14 pair inversions. For candidate *b* to become a Condorcet winner at least 9 voters who are either in group G2 or G3 or G4 must move *b* up two notches in their rankings, i.e., a total of 18 inversions. For candidate *e* to become a Condorcet winner at least 19 voters who are in group G2 must invert $a \succ e$ in their rankings to $e \succ a$, i.e., a total of 19 inversions. As the number of inversions needed to make *a* the Condorcet winner is the smallest, *a* is elected under Dodgson's method.

Now suppose that, *ceteris paribus*, a group (G5) of 10 voters with ranking $a \succ b \succ e \succ c \succ d$ joins the electorate. As a result we obtain the following paired comparison matrix:

	a	*b*	*c*	*d*	*e*
a	–	47	110	89	78
b	63	–	84	89	52
c	0	26	–	78	42
d	21	21	32	–	42
e	32	58	68	68	–

From this matrix it is possible to see that despite the increase in *a*'s support it would still take at least nine voters from group G1 to invert in their rankings $b \succ a$ to $a \succ b$ in order for *a* to become the Condorcet winner, whereas now for *b* to become the Condorcet winner only four voters in Group G4 would have to invert $e \succ a$ to $a \succ e$ in their ranking, and thereafter to invert $e \succ b$ to $b \succ e$—i.e., a total of 8 inversions. So as the number of inversions needed for *b* to become the Condorcet winner is smallest, *b* would be elected under Dodgson's method thereby demonstrating its susceptibility to the P-TOP paradox.

4.9.3 P-BOT + CW

Contrary to the statement made by Felsenthal and Tideman (2013, p. 71, fn 10), Dodgson's procedure is vulnerable to the P-BOT paradox regardless of whether the initial majority method relation contains a top cycle or a Condorcet winner. Here is an example where the initial majority relation contains a Condorcet winner.

Suppose there are nine voters whose preference orderings among four candidates, *a*, *b*, *c*, *d* are as follows:

No. voters	Ranking
5	$b \succ c \succ d \succ a$
4	$c \succ d \succ a \succ b$

Here *b* is the Condorcet winner and as Dodgson's method is Condorcet-consistent *b* is elected.

Now suppose that, *ceteris paribus*, three additional voters whose preference ordering is $a \succ d \succ b \succ c$ join the electorate. As a result the majority method relation contains a top cycle and according to Dodgson's method the candidate who can become a Condorcet winner with fewest preference inversions should be the winner. In the augmented electorate this candidate is *c* because this candidate needs only that three voters invert their preference ordering from $b \succ c$ to $c \succ b$ whereas each of the remaining candidates needs more preference inversions in order to become a Condorcet winner. However, note that here *c* has not been elected initially and was ranked last by the additional voters and despite this has been elected in the enlarged electorate—thereby demonstrating the vulnerability of Dodgson's method to the P-BOT paradox in variable electorates when a Condorcet winner exists initially.

4.9.4 P-BOT + CYC

Suppose there are 11 voters whose preference orderings among four candidates, *a*, *b*, *c*, *d* are as follows:

No. voters	Ranking
5	$b \succ c \succ d \succ a$
4	$c \succ d \succ a \succ b$
2	$a \succ b \succ c \succ d$

Here the majority preference relation is cyclical ($a \succ b \succ c \succ d \succ a$) and *b* is the Dodgson winner because *b* needs only one voter to invert his/her preference ordering from $a \succ b$ to $b \succ a$ in order to become a Condorcet winner whereas each of the other candidates needs more than one preference inversion in order to become a Condorcet winner.

Now suppose that, *ceteris paribus*, three additional voters with preference ordering $d \succ a \succ b \succ c$ join the electorate. As a result the majority preference relation remains cyclical ($a \succ b \succ c \succ d \succ a$) but now candidate c needs only 4 preference inversions in order to become a Condorcet winner (from $b \succ c$ to $c \succ b$) whereas each of the remaining candidates needs more preference inversions to become a Condorcet winner.[11] So the fact that c is elected in the expanded electorate despite the fact that she/he was not elected originally and that the additional voters ranked c at the bottom of their preference ordering demonstrates that Dodgson's method is vulnerable to the P-BOT paradox in variable electorates when the initial majority preference relation is cyclical.

4.10 Types of Monotonicity Failure of Nanson's Method Under Variable Electorates

4.10.1 Impossibility: P-TOP + CW

As Nanson's method is Condorcet-consistent, it cannot display the P-TOP paradox when a Condorcet winner exists initially. This is so because if the Condorcet winner was elected initially then the Condorcet winner will be elected, *a fortiori*, when additional voters join the electorate whose top rank is the Condorcet winner.

4.10.2 P-TOP + CYC

Suppose there are 18 voters whose rankings of four candidates a, b, c, and d, are as follows:

No. of voters	Ranking
5	$a \succ b \succ d \succ c$
5	$b \succ c \succ d \succ a$
6	$c \succ a \succ d \succ b$
1	$c \succ b \succ a \succ d$
1	$c \succ b \succ d \succ a$

[11] For example, in order for b to become a Condorcet winner a total of 5 preference inversions are needed: 3 inversions from $a \succ b$ to $b \succ a$ and another 2 inversions from $d \succ b$ to $b \succ d$.

The majority relation method is cyclical [($a \succ b \succ c \succ a) \succ d$]. The Borda scores of the candidates can be derived from the sum of the lines in the following paired comparison matrix:

	a	*b*	*c*	*d*	Sum
a	–	11	5	12	28
b	7	–	10	12	29
c	13	8	–	13	34
d	6	6	5	–	17
Total					108

The sum of Borda scores of all four candidates is 108, and the average score is 108/4 or 27. So according to the Nanson method, one eliminates at the end of the first counting round candidate *d*, and the re-computed Borda scores for candidates *a*, *b*, and *c*, are 16, 17, and 21, respectively. Since the average of this score is 18, *c* wins.

Now suppose that, *ceteris paribus*, one additional voter with ranking $c \succ b \succ d \succ a$ joins the electorate, thereby *increasing* the number of voters who rank *c* at the top of their ranking. The Borda scores of *a*, *b*, *c*, and *d*, are now 28, 31, 37, and 18, respectively, and the average Borda score is 28.5. Hence according to the Nanson method, candidates *a* and *d* are eliminated in the first count, and candidate *b* beats *c* in the second counting round and is elected—thus demonstrating the susceptibility of Nanson's method to the P-TOP paradox.

4.10.3 *P-BOT + CW*

The same example used in Sect. 4.9.3 to show that Dodgson's method is vulnerable to the P-BOT paradox in variable electorates when the initial social preference ordering contains a Condorcet winner can be used to show that Nanson's method too is vulnerable to this paradox.[12] As Nanson's method is Condorcet-consistent *b* (the Condorcet winner) is elected under Nanson's procedure in the first part of the example. Following the joining of the three $a \succ d \succ b \succ c$ voters (in the second part of the example) one obtains that the Borda scores of candidates *a*, *b*, *c*, *d* are 13, 18, 22, and 19, respectively, and the average score is therefore 18. So according to Nanson's method candidates *a* and *b* are eliminated and thereafter *c* beats *d* (9:3) and becomes the Nanson winner. However, note that here *c* has not been elected initially and was ranked last by the three additional voters and despite this has been

[12]This example and the one in Sect. 4.10.4 refute the statement made by Felsenthal and Tideman (2013, p. 71, fn 10) according to which the Nanson method is invulnerable to the P-BOT paradox in variable electorates.

elected in the enlarged electorate—thereby demonstrating the vulnerability of Nanson's method to the P-BOT paradox in variable electorates when a Condorcet winner exists initially.

4.10.4 P-BOT + CYC

Suppose there are 11 voters whose preference orderings are as follows:

No. voters	Ranking
5	$b \succ c \succ d \succ a$
4	$c \succ d \succ a \succ b$
2	$a \succ d \succ b \succ c$

The social preference ordering is cyclical ($b \succ c \succ d \succ a \succ b$). The Borda scores of candidates *a*, *b*, *c*, *d* are 10, 17, 22, and 17, respectively, and the average Borda score is therefore 16.5. Consequently candidate *a* is eliminated and thereafter the revised Borda scores of candidates *b*, *c*, and *d* are 12, 13, and 8, respectively with an average score of 11. Hence candidate *d* is eliminated and thereafter *b* beats *c* (7:4) and becomes the Nanson winner.

Now suppose that, *ceteris paribus*, one additional voter with preference ordering $d \succ a \succ b \succ c$ joins the electorate. The social preference ordering remains cyclical ($b \succ c \succ d \succ a \succ b$). The Borda scores of candidates *a*, *b*, *c*, *d* are now 12, 18, 22, and 20, respectively, and the average Borda score is therefore 18. Consequently candidates *a* and *b* are eliminated and thereafter *c* beats *d* (9:3) and becomes the Nanson winner. However, note that *c* was not elected initially and was ranked last by the additional voter. Despite this *c* is elected according to Nanson's method thereby showing that this procedure is vulnerable to the P-BOT paradox when the initial preference ordering contains a cycle.

4.11 Summary and Conclusions

Table 4.1 summarizes the types of monotonicity failure that are displayed by our examples of monotonicity failure in both fixed and variable electorates under each of the five investigated voting methods in this chapter. 'Yes' means that that type of monotonicity failure was displayed by an example we provided, and 'No' means we explained why no such example exists.

On the basis of this table we can say that, a priori, of the five methods investigated in this chapter, the Plurality with Runoff, the Alternative Vote and Coombs methods–two of which are used in practice in public elections—are vulnerable to more sub-types of

Table 4.1 Summary

Sub-type	Method				
	Plurality with Runoff	Alternative Vote	Coombs	Dodgson	Nanson
[U+CW+B]	Yes	Yes	Yes	No	No
[U+CW+W]	Yes	Yes	No	No	No
[U+CYC+B]	Yes	Yes	Yes	No	Yes
[U+CYC+W]	Yes	Yes	No	Yes	Yes
[D+CW+B]	Yes	Yes	Yes	No	No
[D+CW+W]	No	No	Yes	No	No
[D+CYC+B]	Yes	Yes	Yes	Yes	Yes
[D+CYC+W]	No	No	Yes	No	Yes
P-TOP+CW+W	No	No	Yes	No	No
P-TOP+CYC+W	No	No	Yes	Yes	Yes
P-BOT+CW+W	Yes	Yes	No	Yes	Yes
P-BOT+CYC+W	Yes	Yes	No	Yes	Yes

monotonicity failure when the electorate is fixed than Dodgson's and Nanson's methods. On the other hand, both the Plurality with Runoff and the Alternative Vote methods are not at all vulnerable to the P-TOP paradox when the electorate is variable, while the Coombs method is more vulnerable to this paradox than either the Dodgson or the Nanson methods. However, of the five methods investigated in this chapter, Coombs' method is the only one which is not susceptible to the P-BOT paradox when the electorate is variable.

If we look, under fixed electorates, only on the four subtypes [U+B], [U+W], [D+B] and [D+W] then on the basis of Table 4.1 we can say that, a priori, of the five investigated voting methods in this chapter Nanson's method is vulnerable to all four sub-types of monotonicity failure, while Dodgson's method is vulnerable to only two of them. P-R and AV—both of which are used in practice in public elections—are vulnerable to three of the sub-types. Perhaps somewhat surprisingly, sub-type [D+B] afflicts all the five investigated methods, while sub-type [D+W] afflicts only two of the methods (which are not used in practice in public elections).

References

Felsenthal, D. S., & Maoz, Z. (1992). Normative properties of four single-stage multi-winner electoral procedures. *Behavioral Science, 37,* 109–127.

Felsenthal, D. S., & Tideman, N. (2013). Varieties of failure of monotonicity and participation under five voting methods. *Theory and Decision, 75,* 59–77.

Felsenthal, D. S., & Tideman, N. (2014). Interacting double monotonicity failure with direction of impact under five voting methods. *Mathematical Social Sciences, 67,* 57–66.

Fishburn, P. C. (1977). Condorcet social choice functions. *SIAM Journal of Applied Mathematics, 33,* 469–489.

Fishburn, P. C., & Brams, S. J. (1983). Paradoxes of preferential voting. *Mathematics Magazine, 56,* 207–214.

Miller, N. R. (2012). Monotonicity failure in IRV elections with three candidates. Paper presented at the Second World Congress of the Public Choice Societies, Miami, FL, March 8–11, 2012. Downloadable from http://userpages.umbc.edu/~nmiller/MF&IRV.pdf

Chapter 5
Eight Voting Rules Susceptible to Types of Monotonicity Failure Under Variable Electorates

Abstract This chapter expands the illustration and analysis regarding the susceptibility of eight voting procedures to two types of what are generally known as No-Show paradoxes. Following the article by Felsenthal and Tideman (2013), the two paradoxes are denoted as P-TOP and P-BOT paradoxes. According to the P-TOP paradox it is possible that if candidate x has been elected by a given electorate then, *ceteris paribus*, another candidate, y, may be elected if additional voters join the electorate who rank x at the *top* of their preference ordering. Similarly, according to the P-BOT paradox it is possible that if candidate y has *not* been elected by a given electorate then, *ceteris paribus*, y may be elected if additional voters join the electorate who rank y at the *bottom* of their preference ordering. Voting procedures that are susceptible to these paradoxes are considered to be afflicted with a particularly serious defect because instead of encouraging voters to participate in an election and vote according to their true preference orderings, they may inhibit voters from participating in an election and thereby undermine the rationale for conducting elections.

Keywords Elections · No-show paradoxes · Non-monotonicity · Voting paradoxes · Voting methods · Voting procedures

5.1 Introduction

In this chapter we shall demonstrate types of monotonicity failures under variable electorates to which the eight voting procedures described in Sect. 2.3 are susceptible. As in the previous chapter, monotonicity failures under variable electorates require an increase in the original electorate in order to demonstrate two possible paradoxes. The first paradox arises if one of the candidates, say candidate x, has been elected initially, then it is possible that another candidate, y, will be elected if, *ceteris paribus*, *the electorate is increased* as a result of additional voters

This chapter is largely based on Felsenthal and Nurmi (2016)

D.S. Felsenthal and H. Nurmi, *Monotonicity Failures Afflicting Procedures for Electing a Single Candidate*, SpringerBriefs in Economics,
DOI 10.1007/978-3-319-51061-3_5

whose *top-ranked* candidate is x join the electorate. The second paradox arises if one of the candidates, say candidate z, has not been elected initially, then it is possible that candidate z will be elected if, *ceteris paribus*, *the electorate is increased* as a result of additional voters whose *bottom-ranked* candidate is z join the electorate. We denote the first paradox as P-TOP and the second as P-BOT. Obviously the dynamic (added) voters are worse off under both paradoxes. So we only distinguish between initial situations where a Condorcet winner (CW) exists and situations where the social preference ordering includes a top cycle (CYC).

5.2 Types of Monotonicity Failure of the Successive Elimination Method Under Variable Electorate

5.2.1 Impossibility: P-TOP + CW

As the Successive Elimination method is Condorcet-consistent, it cannot display the P-TOP paradox when a Condorcet winner exists initially. This is so because if the Condorcet winner was elected initially then the Condorcet winner will be elected, *a fortiori*, when additional voters join the electorate whose top rank is the Condorcet winner.

5.2.2 P-TOP + CYC

This example is due to Moulin (1988, p. 54). Suppose there are six voters who must elect one of three candidates *a, b,* or *c* under the Successive Elimination method, and that their preference orderings are as follows:

No. of voters	Preference orderings
2	$a \succ b \succ c$
2	$b \succ c \succ a$
1	$c \succ a \succ b$
1	$c \succ b \succ a$

Here the social preference ordering is cyclical ($b \succ c \succ a \sim b$). Assume further that: (1) the first voting round is between a and b, and the second voting round is between the winner of the first round and c; (2) all voters vote sincerely in both voting rounds; and (3) if a tie occurs in any voting round it is broken lexicographically.

Accordingly, in the first round there is a tie between *a* and *b* which is broken in favor of *a*, and in the second round *c* beats *a* (4:2) and, hence, *c* is the ultimate winner.

Now assume that, *ceteris paribus*, an additional voter whose preference ordering is $c \succ b \succ a$ joins the electorate. In consequence, *b* will beat *a* (4:3) in the first round and *b* will beat *c* (4:3) in the second round—and thus *b* becomes the ultimate winner, thereby demonstrating the susceptibility of the Successive Elimination procedure to the P-TOP paradox.

5.2.3 *P-BOT + CW*

Suppose there are nine voters who must elect one of four candidates *a, b, c, d* under the Successive Elimination method, and that their preference orderings are as follows:

No. of Voters	Preference orderings
5	$b \succ c \succ d \succ a$
4	$c \succ d \succ a \succ b$

Assume further that:

(1) The first voting round is between *a* and *b*, the second voting round is between the winner of the first round and *c*, and the third round is between the winner of the second round and *d*.
(2) All voters vote sincerely in all voting rounds.

Accordingly, as *b* is ranked first by an absolute majority of the voters (and hence is also the Condorcet winner), this candidate will be the ultimate winner regardless of the order in which the various candidates are voted upon.

Now assume that, *ceteris paribus*, three additional voters whose preference ordering is $a \succ d \succ b \succ c$ join the electorate. As a result, *a* will beat *b* (7:5) in the first round, *c* will beat *a* (9:3) in the second round, and *c* will beat *d* (9:3) in the third round—and thus *c* becomes the ultimate winner, thereby demonstrating the susceptibility of the Successive Elimination procedure to the P-BOT paradox.

5.2.4 *P-BOT + CYC*

Suppose there are nine voters who must elect one of four candidates *a, b, c, d* under the Successive Elimination method, and that their preference orderings are as follows:

No. of Voters	Preference orderings
3	$b \succ c \succ d \succ a$
2	$d \succ b \succ c \succ a$
4	$c \succ d \succ a \succ b$

The social preference ordering here contains a top cycle (b $\succ c \succ d \succ b) \succ a$. Assume further that:

(1) The first voting round is between *a* and *b*, the second voting round is between the winner of the first round and *c*, and the third round is between the winner of the second round and *d*.
(2) All voters vote sincerely in all voting rounds.

Accordingly, *b* beats *a* in the first round and *b* beats *c* in the second round and *d* beats *b* in the third round, and hence *d* is the ultimate winner.

Now assume that, *ceteris paribus*, three additional voters whose preference ordering is $a \succ d \succ b \succ c$ join the electorate. As a result, *a* will beat *b* (7:5) in the first round, *c* will beat *a* (9:3) in the second round, and *c* will beat *d* (7:5) in the third round—and thus *c* becomes the ultimate winner, thereby demonstrating the susceptibility of the Successive Elimination procedure to the P-BOT paradox.

5.3 Types of Monotonicity Failure of Bucklin's Method Under Variable Electorate

5.3.1 P-TOP + CW

Suppose there are five voters who must elect one of six candidates *a, b, c, d, x, y* under Bucklin's method, and that their preference orderings are as follows:

No. of voters	Preference orderings
1	$a \succ c \succ x \succ b \succ d \succ y$
1	$a \succ d \succ x \succ b \succ c \succ y$
1	$b \succ d \succ x \succ a \succ c \succ y$
1	$b \succ y \succ x \succ a \succ c \succ d$
1	$c \succ y \succ x \succ a \succ b \succ d$

Here *x* is the Condorcet winner. However, as can easily be seen from this table, no candidate constitutes the top preference of an absolute majority of the voters nor of the top and second preferences of the majority of voters. However, since

x constitutes the third preference of all voters, x is elected in this example according to Bucklin's method.

Now suppose that, *ceteris paribus*, two additional voters whose preference orderings are $x \succ y \succ a \succ b \succ c \succ d$ join the electorate, thereby, presumably, strengthening x's position. However, in fact, candidate y will now be elected according to Bucklin's method—thereby demonstrating the vulnerability of this method to the P-TOP paradox—because this candidate constitutes the second preference of a majority (4) of voters, whereas for x to continue being the winner one must take into consideration not only the voters' top two preferences but also their third preference.

5.3.2 P-TOP + CYC

Suppose there are six voters who must elect one of six candidates *a, b, c, d, x, y* under Bucklin's method, and that their preference orderings are as follows:

No. of voters	Preference orderings
1	$a \succ c \succ x \succ b \succ d \succ y$
1	$a \succ d \succ x \succ b \succ c \succ y$
1	$b \succ d \succ x \succ a \succ c \succ y$
1	$b \succ y \succ x \succ a \succ c \succ d$
1	$c \succ y \succ x \succ a \succ b \succ d$
1	$y \succ d \succ c \succ b \succ a \succ x$

Here the social preference ordering is cyclical ($a \succ c \succ y \sim a \succ d \sim x \sim b \succ y \sim a$). As can easily be seen from this table, no candidate constitutes the top preference of an absolute majority of the voters nor of the top and second preferences of the majority of voters. However, since x constitutes the third preference of all voters, x is elected in this example according to Bucklin's method.

Now suppose that, *ceteris paribus*, two additional voters whose preference orderings are $x \succ y \succ a \succ b \succ c \succ d$ join the electorate, thereby, presumably, strengthening x's position. However, in fact, candidate y will now be elected according to Bucklin's method—thereby demonstrating the vulnerability of this method to the P-TOP paradox—because this candidate constitutes the first and second preference of a majority (5) of voters, whereas for x to continue being the winner one must take into consideration not only the voters' top two preferences but also their third preference.

5.3.3 P-BOT + CW

Suppose there are nine voters who must elect one of four candidates *a, b, c, d* under Bucklin's method, and that their preference orderings are as in the first part of Sect. 5.2.3. As *b* is ranked first by an absolute majority of the voters (and hence is also the Condorcet winner), *b* will be elected under Bucklin's procedure.

Now assume that, as in the second part of Sect. 5.2.3, three additional voters whose preference ordering is $a \succ d \succ b \succ c$ join the electorate. As a result, *c*—who was not elected in the original electorate and who is ranked last by the additional voters—is now elected under Bucklin's method because the number of voters (9) who rank *c* as their top and second preference exceeds the number of voters who rank any of the other candidates in their top and second preference, thereby demonstrating the susceptibility of Bucklin's procedure to the P-BOT paradox.

5.3.4 P-BOT + CYC

Suppose there are nine voters who must elect one of six candidates *a, b, c, d, e, f* under Bucklin's method, and that their preference orderings are as follows:

No. of Voters	Preference orderings
3	$b \succ f \succ c \succ e \succ d \succ a$
4	$c \succ e \succ d \succ a \succ f \succ b$
2	$d \succ b \succ f \succ c \succ e \succ a$

The social preference ordering here is cyclical $[(f \succ c \succ e \succ d \succ b \succ f) \succ a]$. Since no alternative is ranked first by a majority of the voters one looks also on the voters' second preferences. Consequently we see that *b* constitutes the first and second preferences of 5 voters who constitute a majority of the voters, hence *b* is elected according to Bucklin's procedure in this example.

Now suppose that, *ceteris paribus*, one voter whose preference ordering is $a \succ f \succ e \succ b \succ d \succ c$ joins the electorate. As a result *c* wins with 7 first and third preferences—a larger majority than that obtained by any of the other candidates at this counting stage, this despite the fact that *c* was ranked last by the additional voter—thereby demonstrating the susceptibility of Bucklin's method to the P-BOT paradox when the initial social choice preference is cyclical.

5.4 Types of Monotonicity Failure of the Majority Judgment (MJ) Method Under Variable Electorate

5.4.1 P-TOP + CW

Suppose that three voters, $V_1 - V_3$, grade two candidates, *x* and *y*, on an ordinal scale ranging between A (lowest) and D (highest), as follows:

Candidate/Voter	V_1	V_2	V_3	Median grade
x	B	D	D	D
y	C	C	C	C

Since the median grade (D) of candidate *x* exceeds that of candidate *y*, candidate *x* (who is also the Condorcet winner) is elected according to the MJ procedure.

Now suppose that, *ceteris paribus*, two additional voters, V_4 and V_5, join the electorate assigning to candidates *x* and *y* the ranks B and A, respectively. As a result, we get:

Candidate/Voter	V_1	V_2	V_3	V_4	V_5	Median grade
x	B	D	D	B	B	B
y	C	C	C	A	A	C

Here *y* is the winner according to the MJ procedure because *y*'s median grade (C) is higher than that of *x*; thus the two additional voters caused their more favorite candidate, *x*, not to be elected even though they awarded *x* a higher grade than they awarded *y*—which demonstrates the susceptibility of the MJ procedure to the P-TOP paradox. However, it should be noted that a necessary condition for the MJ procedure to display the P-TOP paradox when there are only two candidates is that the grade awarded by the additional voters to the original winner must be lower than his/her median grade in the original situation. The same is true of its vulnerability to the P-BOT paradox, as will be seen shortly.

5.4.2 P-TOP + CYC

Suppose that three voters, $V_1 - V_3$, grade three candidates, *x*, *y*, and *z*, on an ordinal scale ranging between A (lowest) and E (highest), as follows:

Candidate/Voter	V_1	V_2	V_3	Median grade
x	A	D	B	B
y	C	A	C	C
z	E	B	A	B

The social preference ordering here is cyclical ($y \succ x \succ z \succ y$). Since the median grade (C) of candidate y is highest, this candidate is elected according to the MJ procedure.

Now suppose that, *ceteris paribus*, two additional voters, V_4 and V_5, join the electorate and assign to alternatives x, y, and z the ranks D,E, and A, respectively. As a result we get:

Candidate/Voter	V_1	V_2	V_3	V_4	V_5	Median grade
x	A	D	B	D	D	D
y	C	A	C	E	E	C
z	E	B	A	A	A	A

Here x becomes the winner according to the MJ procedure despite the fact that the two additional voters assigned to y (the previous winner) the highest rank—thereby demonstrating the susceptibility of the MJ procedure to the P-TOP paradox when the initial preference ordering is cyclical.

5.4.3 *P-BOT + CW*

This example is adapted from Felsenthal and Machover (2008, p. 329). Suppose that five voters, $V_1 - V_5$, grade two candidates, x and y, on an ordinal scale ranging between A (lowest) and F (highest), as follows:

Candidate/Voter	V_1	V_2	V_3	V_4	V_5	Median grade
x	A	D	E	E	F	E
y	B	C	F	F	F	F

Since the median grade (F) of candidate y is higher than that of candidate x, candidate y (who is also the Condorcet winner) is elected according to the MJ procedure.

Given that candidate x has not been elected, suppose now that, *ceteris paribus*, two additional voters, V_6 and V_7, join the electorate, assigning to candidates x and y the same (or similar) grades as those assigned by voter V_1 (i.e., the lowest grade to x and a higher grade to y not exceeding C). As a result, we get:

Candidate/Voter	V_1	V_2	V_3	V_4	V_5	V_6	V_7	Median grade
x	A	D	E	E	F	A	A	D
y	B	C	F	F	F	B	B	C

Here *x* is the winner according to the MJ procedure because *x*'s median grade (D) is higher than that of *y*; the two additional voters thus caused their less favorite candidate, *x*, to be elected even though they assigned to *x* the lowest grade possible—which demonstrates the susceptibility of the MJ procedure to the P-BOT paradox.

5.4.4 P-BOT + CYC

Suppose that five voters, $V_1 - V_5$, grade three candidates, *x, y*, and *z* on an ordinal scale ranging between A (lowest) and I (highest), as follows:

Candidate/Voter	V_1	V_2	V_3	V_4	V_5	Median grade
x	C	F	G	G	G	G
y	D	C	H	H	H	H
z	B	E	A	I	I	E

Here the social preference ordering is cyclical ($y \succ x \succ z \succ y$). Since the median grade (H) of candidate *y* is higher than that of the other two candidates, candidate *y* is elected according to the MJ procedure.

Given that candidate *x* has not been elected, suppose now that, *ceteris paribus*, two additional voters, V_6 and V_7, join the electorate, assigning to candidates *x, y*, and *z* grades A, B, and B, respectively. As a result, we get:

Candidate/Voter	V_1	V_2	V_3	V_4	V_5	V_6	V_7	Median grade
x	C	F	G	G	G	A	A	F
y	D	C	H	H	H	B	B	D
z	B	E	A	I	I	B	B	B

Here *x* is the winner according to the MJ procedure because *x*'s median grade (F) is higher than that of the other two candidates; the two additional voters thus caused their less favorite candidate, *x*, to be elected even though they assigned to *x* the lowest grade possible—which demonstrates the susceptibility of the MJ procedure to the P-BOT paradox when the initial social preference ordering is cyclical.

5.5 Types of Monotonicity Failure of Copeland's Method Under Variable Electorate

5.5.1 *Impossibility: P-TOP + CW*

As Copeland's method is Condorcet-consistent, it cannot display the P-TOP paradox when a Condorcet winner exists initially. This is so because if the Condorcet winner was elected initially then the Condorcet winner will be elected, *a fortiori*, when additional voters join the electorate whose top rank is the Condorcet winner.

5.5.2 *P-TOP + CYC*

This example is adapted from Richelson (1978, p. 174), who copied it from an example used by Fishburn (1977, p. 483) in a somewhat different context.

Assume there are four voters who must select one out of five candidates, *a, b, c, d, e*, whose preference orderings over these candidates are as follows:

No. of voters	Preference orderings
2	$e \succ d \succ a \succ b \succ c$
1	$c \succ b \succ a \succ e \succ d$
1	$d \succ c \succ b \succ a \succ e$

The social preference ordering here is cyclical ($e \succ d \succ a \sim b \sim c \sim e$). This preference list can be transformed into the following paired comparisons matrix.

	a	*b*	*c*	*d*	*e*
a	–	2	2	1	2
b	2	–	2	1	2
c	2	2	–	1	2
d	3	3	3	–	1
e	2	2	2	3	–

From this matrix we can see that according to Copeland's procedure, each of candidates *a,b* and *c* gets 1.5 points (since each of these three candidates ties with three other candidates and loses to one candidate), candidate *e* gets 2.5 points (since this candidate ties with three other candidates and beats one candidate),while candidate *d* gets 3 points (because it beats three candidates and is beaten by one candidate). So according to Copeland's procedure *d* is the winner.

Now suppose that, *ceteris paribus*, an additional voter with preference ordering $d \succ e \succ a \succ b \succ c$ joins the electorate. One thus could expect, presumably, that the chances of candidate *d* being elected would increase. However, as a result of this expansion of the electorate, candidate *e* becomes the Condorcet winner and, hence, elected according to Copeland's procedure—thereby demonstrating the susceptibility of this procedure to the P-TOP paradox.

5.5.3 P-BOT + CW

Suppose there are nine voters who must elect one of four candidates, *a, b, c, d*, under Copeland's method, and that their preference orderings are as in the first part of Sect. 5.2.3. As *b* is ranked first by an absolute majority of the voters (and who is therefore also the Condorcet winner), *b* will be elected under Copeland's procedure.

Now assume that, as in the second part of Sect. 5.2.3, three additional voters whose preference ordering is $a \succ d \succ b \succ c$ join the electorate. As a result, the social preference ordering becomes cyclical ($a \succ b \succ c \succ d \succ a$); thus, according to Copeland's procedure only *c* and *d* (each with two points) should belong to the choice set. Hence *c*—who was not elected in the original electorate and who is ranked last by the additional voters—now belongs to the choice set according to Copeland's procedure, thereby demonstrating the susceptibility of Copeland's procedure to the P-BOT paradox when a Condorcet winner exists initially.

5.5.4 P-BOT + CYC

Suppose there are nine voters who must elect one of six candidates, *a, b, c, d, e, f* under Copeland's method, and that their preference orderings are as follows:

No. of voters	Preference orderings
3	$b \succ f \succ c \succ e \succ d \succ a$
4	$c \succ e \succ d \succ a \succ f \succ b$
2	$d \succ b \succ f \succ c \succ e \succ a$

Here the social preference ordering contains a top cycle $[(f \succ c \succ e \succ d \succ b \succ f) \succ a]$ and the unique Copeland winner is *b* (with 4 points).

Now assume that, *ceteris paribus*, three additional voters whose preference ordering is $a \succ d \succ f \succ e \succ b \succ c$ join the electorate. As a result there is a tie according to Copeland's method between *c, d, e,* and *f* (each with 3 points), thus *c*, who constitutes the last preference of the additional voters belongs to the winning set—thereby demonstrating the vulnerability of the Copeland method to the P-BOT paradox when the initial preference ordering contains a top cycle.

5.6 Types of Monotonicity Failure of Black's Method Under Variable Electorate

5.6.1 Impossibility: P-TOP + CW

As Black's method is Condorcet-consistent, it cannot display the P-TOP paradox when a Condorcet winner exists initially. This is so because if the Condorcet winner was elected initially then the Condorcet winner will be elected, *a fortiori*, when additional voters join the electorate whose top rank is the Condorcet winner.

5.6.2 P-TOP + CYC

The vulnerability of Black's procedure to the P-TOP paradox has been demonstrated by Richelson (1978, p. 174) using an example in which the initial electorate contains four voters and six candidates. The example below seems to us to be somewhat simpler.

Assume there are 14 voters who must select one out of five candidates, *a, b, c, d, e*, whose preference orderings over these candidates are as follows:

No. of voters	Preference orderings
3	$d \succ e \succ a \succ b \succ c$
3	$e \succ a \succ c \succ b \succ d$
4	$c \succ d \succ e \succ a \succ b$
3	$d \succ e \succ b \succ c \succ a$
1	$e \succ b \succ a \succ d \succ c$

This preference list can be depicted as the following paired comparisons matrix:

	a	*b*	*c*	*d*	*e*	Sum
a	–	10	7	4	0	21
b	4	–	7	4	0	15
c	7	7	–	7	4	25
d	10	10	7	–	10	37
e	14	14	10	4	–	42

According to Black's method, the Condorcet winner, if one exists, should be elected; otherwise the winner is elected according to Borda's method. As one can see from the above matrix of paired comparisons, the social preference ordering in the example is cyclical ($a \succ b \sim c \sim d \succ e \succ a$), so the winner must be elected according to Borda's method. The Borda scores of candidates *a, b, c, d,* and *e,* can be computed as the sums of the rows of the above matrix, which are 21, 15, 25, 37, and 42, respectively, so *e* is the Borda winner.

Now suppose that, *ceteris paribus*, two additional voters with preference ordering $e \succ b \succ a \succ d \succ c$ join the electorate. As a result, we obtain the following revised matrix of paired comparisons:

	a	*b*	*c*	*d*	*e*
a	–	10	9	6	0
b	6	–	9	6	0
c	7	7	–	7	4
d	10	10	9	–	10
e	16	16	12	6	–

As one can see from this matrix, all of the numbers in *d*'s row are larger than half the number of voters. Hence, *d* becomes the Condorcet winner and is therefore elected according to Black's method—thereby demonstrating the vulnerability of this method to the P-TOP paradox.

5.6.3 *P-BOT + CW*

Suppose there are nine voters who must elect one of four candidates *a, b, c, d* under Black's method, and that their preference orderings are as in the first part of Sect. 5.2.3. As *b* is ranked first by an absolute majority of the voters and, hence, is the Condorcet winner, *b* will be elected under Black's procedure.

Now assume that, as in the second part of Sect. 5.2.3, three additional voters whose preference ordering is $a \succ d \succ b \succ c$ join the electorate. As a result, the social preference ordering becomes cyclical ($a \succ b \succ c \succ d \succ a$); so, according to Black's procedure one uses Borda's method to determine the winner. According to Borda's method the number of points awarded to candidates *a, b, c, d* is 13, 18, 22, and 19, respectively. Despite the fact that *c* was not elected in the original electorate and was ranked last by the additional voters who joined the electorate, *c* nevertheless is elected in the expanded electorate according to Black's procedure, again demonstrating the vulnerability of this procedure to the P-BOT paradox.

5.6.4 *Impossibility: P-BOT + CYC*

If the social preference ordering is cyclical at the outset, then the Black winner has to be the Borda winner. Suppose this Borda winner is not x. However, adding one or more voters whose least-preferred candidate is x cannot make x either the Borda winner (if the social preference ordering continues to be cyclical) or turn x into being a Condorcet winner if x was not initially the Condorcet winner. Hence it is impossible to demonstrate the P-BOT paradox under Black's procedure when the initial social preference ordering is cyclical.

5.7 Types of Monotonicity Failure of Kemeny's Method Under Variable Electorate

5.7.1 *Impossibility: P-TOP + CW*

As Kemeny's method is Condorcet-consistent, it cannot display the P-TOP paradox when a Condorcet winner exists initially. This is so because if the Condorcet winner was elected initially then the Condorcet winner will be elected, *a fortiori*, when additional voters join the electorate whose top rank is the Condorcet winner.

5.7.2 *P-TOP + CYC*

The vulnerability of Kemeny's method to the P-TOP paradox can be demonstrated by using an example constructed by Fishburn (1977, p. 484) for another purpose. It involved nine candidates—and hence the need to examine 9! possible preference orderings. Thus the following 4-candidate example is considerably simpler.

Assume there are 15 voters who must select one out of four candidates, *a, b, c, d,* and whose preference orderings among these candidates are as follows:

No. of voters	Preference orderings
5	$d \succ b \succ c \succ a$
4	$b \succ c \succ a \succ d$
3	$a \succ d \succ c \succ b$
3	$a \succ d \succ b \succ c$

This preference list can be transformed into the following paired comparisons matrix:

	a	*b*	*c*	*d*
a	–	6	6	10
b	9	–	12	4
c	9	3	–	4
d	5	11	11	–

As one can see from the matrix, the social preference ordering is cyclical ($d \succ b \succ c \succ a \succ d$). So, according to Kemeny's procedure, out of the 4! = 24 possible (strict and transitive) social preference orderings, the most likely one is $d \succ b \succ c \succ a$ because the sum of 57 (=11 + 11 + 5 + 12 + 9 + 9) associated with the six pairwise comparisons of this social preference ordering is highest. Thus, according to Kemeny's method *d* will be elected.

Now suppose that, *ceteris paribus*, four additional voters whose preference ordering is $d \succ a \succ b \succ c$ join the electorate. We then obtain the following revised matrix of paired comparisons:

	a	*b*	*c*	*d*
a	–	10	10	10
b	9	–	16	4
c	9	3	–	4
d	9	15	15	–

As one can see from this revised matrix, *a* becomes the Condorcet winner and is therefore elected under Kemeny's method—thereby demonstrating the vulnerability of Kemeny's method to the P-TOP paradox.

5.7.3 P-BOT + CW

Assume there are 11 voters who must select one out of four candidates, *a, b, c, d*, and that their preference orderings among these candidates are as follows:

No. of voters	Preference orderings
5	$d \succ b \succ c \succ a$
3	$a \succ d \succ c \succ b$
3	$a \succ d \succ b \succ c$

Here, a (who is ranked first by an absolute majority of the voters) is the Condorcet winner, so a is elected according to Kemeny's procedure.

Now suppose that, *ceteris paribus*, four additional voters whose preference ordering is $b \succ c \succ a \succ d$ join the electorate. As a result we obtain the same paired comparisons matrix as in the first part of Sect. 5.7.2, i.e., we obtain that the social preference ordering becomes cyclical ($a \succ d \succ b \succ c \succ a$) and, hence, according to Kemeny's procedure, the most likely (transitive) social preference ordering is $d \succ b \succ c \succ a$ because the sum (57) associated with the pairwise comparisons of this social preference ordering is highest. Thus, according to Kemeny's method d will be elected—thereby demonstrating the vulnerability of that method to the P-BOT paradox.

5.7.4 P-BOT + CYC

Assume there are 13 voters who must select one out of four candidates, *a, b, c, d*, and that their preference orderings among these candidates are as follows:

No. of voters	Preference orderings
5	$d \succ b \succ c \succ a$
3	$a \succ d \succ c \succ b$
3	$a \succ d \succ b \succ c$
2	$b \succ c \succ a \succ d$

Here the social preference ordering is cyclical ($a \succ d \succ b \succ c \succ a$) and the most likely (transitive) social preference ordering is $a \succ d \succ b \succ c$ because the sum (52) associated with the pairwise comparisons of this social preference ordering is highest.

Now suppose that, *ceteris paribus*, four additional voters whose preference ordering is $b \succ c \succ a \succ d$ join the electorate. The social preference ordering remains cyclical ($a \succ d \succ b \succ c \succ a$) and as a result we obtain that the most likely (transitive) social preference ordering is $d \succ b \succ c \succ a$ because the sum (63) associated with the pairwise comparisons of this social preference ordering is highest. Thus, according to Kemeny's method *d*, who is ranked last by the additional voters, will be elected—thereby demonstrating the vulnerability of Kemeny's method to the P-BOT paradox when the initial social preference ordering contains a top cycle.

5.8 Types of Monotonicity Failure of Schwartz's Method Under Variable Electorate

5.8.1 *Impossibility: P-TOP + CW*

As Schwartz's method is Condorcet-consistent, it cannot display the P-TOP paradox when a Condorcet winner exists initially. This is so because if the Condorcet winner was elected initially then the Condorcet winner will be elected, *a fortiori*, when additional voters join the electorate whose top rank is the Condorcet winner.

5.8.2 *P-TOP + CYC*

Here we use a slightly revised definition of the P-TOP paradox, wherein a candidate, x, who belongs to a *set* of winners in the original electorate, becomes a loser if, *ceteris paribus*, an additional voter joins the electorate who ranks x at the top of his/her preference ordering.

Assume there are six voters who have to select one of four candidates, *a, b, c, d* according to Schwartz's procedure and whose preference orderings are as follows:

No. of voters	Preference orderings
1	$a \succ c \succ b \succ d$
1	$b \succ d \succ a \succ c$
1	$c \succ b \succ d \succ a$
1	$d \succ a \succ c \succ b$
2	$d \succ c \succ a \succ b$

This preference list can be transformed into the following paired comparisons matrix:

	a	b	c	d
a	–	4	3	1
b	2	–	1	3
c	3	5	–	2
d	5	3	4	–

The social preference ordering here is cyclical ($d \succ a \sim c \succ b \sim d$); according to Schwartz's procedure, all four candidates should belong to the choice set.

Now suppose that, *ceteris paribus*, one additional voter joins the electorate whose preference ordering is $a \succ d \succ c \succ b$. Since a's position is presumably strengthened, one would expect that *a* would continue to belong to the choice set. However, as a result of this expansion of the electorate, *d* becomes the Condorcet winner and is therefore elected according to Schwartz's procedure—thereby demonstrating the vulnerability of this procedure to the P-TOP paradox.

5.8.3 P-BOT + CW

Here, too, we use a somewhat revised definition of the P-BOT paradox. According to this, a P-BOT paradox occurs whenever candidate *x* is the *unique* winner in the original electorate and, after an additional group of voters ranking another candidate *y* at the *bottom* of their preference orderings joins the electorate, the outcome is a tie that includes candidate *y*.

Suppose there are nine voters who must elect one of four candidates *a, b, c, d* under Schwartz's method, and that their preference orderings are as in the first part of Sect. 5.2.3. As *b* is ranked first by an absolute majority of the voters, *b* will be elected under Schwartz's procedure.

Now assume that, as in the second part of Sect. 5.2.3, three additional voters whose preference ordering is $a \succ d \succ b \succ c$ join the electorate. As a result the social preference ordering becomes cyclical ($a \succ b \succ c \succ d \succ a$); according to Schwartz's procedure, all four candidates should belong to the choice set—including *c*, who was not elected in the original electorate and was ranked last by the additional voters who joined the electorate, thereby demonstrating the vulnerability of Schwartz's procedure to the P-BOT paradox.

5.8.4 Impossibility: P-BOT + CYC

Schwartz's method cannot display the P-BOT paradox when the initial social preference ordering is cyclical. This is so because:

1. If the initial cyclic profile is followed, as a result of the entry of additional voters, by one with a CW, then the CW cannot be the last ranked alternative of the additional voters because these voters bring no additional votes to their bottom ranked alternative in any pairwise contest.
2. If the cyclic profile is followed by another cyclic profile consisting of the same alternatives, then it is equally clear that the new profile winners cannot include the last ranked alternative of the new entrants (unless it was in the choice set originally).
3. If the original profile is followed by one where the choice set is a proper subset of the original one, then this cannot include the last ranked alternative of the new entrants since this alternative does not beat or tie with any other with higher majority threshold if it did not do so originally.

4. The case where the Schwartz choice set expands with the new voters joining to include also their bottom preference is impossible because, as stated in (1), the additional voters contribute no additional votes to their bottom-ranked alternative in any pairwise contest.

5.9 Types of Monotonicity Failure of Young's Method Under Variable Electorate

5.9.1 Impossibility: P-TOP + CW

As Young's method is Condorcet-consistent, it cannot display the P-TOP paradox when a Condorcet winner exists initially. This is so because if the Condorcet winner was elected initially then the Condorcet winner will be elected, *a fortiori*, when additional voters join the electorate whose top rank is the Condorcet winner.

5.9.2 P-TOP + CYC

This example is adapted from an example used by Pérez (2001, p. 609) for another purpose.

Suppose there are 39 voters whose preference orderings among five candidates, *a, b, c, d, e*, are as follows:

No. of voters	Preference orderings	No. of voters	Preference orderings
11	$b \succ a \succ d \succ e \succ c$	2	$e \succ d \succ c \succ b \succ a$
10	$e \succ c \succ b \succ d \succ a$	2	$c \succ b \succ a \succ d \succ e$
10	$a \succ c \succ d \succ b \succ e$	1	$d \succ c \succ b \succ a \succ e$
2	$e \succ c \succ d \succ b \succ a$	1	$a \succ b \succ d \succ e \succ c$

These preference orderings can be transformed into the following paired comparisons matrix:

	a	*b*	*c*	*d*	*e*
a	–	11	22	24	25
b	28	–	12	24	25
c	17	27	–	24	13
d	15	15	15	–	25
e	14	14	26	14	–

As one can see from this matrix, the social preference ordering here is cyclical ($c \succ b \succ a \succ d \succ e \succ c$). The minimal number of voters one must remove in order for any of the five candidates to become a Condorcet winner is 12 (the ten voters whose top preference is *a* and the two voters whose top preference is *c*) in order for *e* to become the Condorcet winner. So, *e* is elected according to Young's procedure given this profile.

Now suppose that, *ceteris paribus*, ten new voters whose preference ordering is $e \succ d \succ a \succ b \succ c$ join the electorate—thus presumably strengthening *e*'s position. However, as a result of this expansion of the electorate *d* becomes the Condorcet winner and is therefore elected according to Young's procedure—thereby demonstrating the susceptibility of this procedure to the P-TOP paradox.

5.9.3 Impossibility: P-BOT

Joaquin Pérez (2001, p. 614) supplied the following argument according to which Young's method is invulnerable to the P-BOT paradox.

Suppose we start with a profile P of voters' preferences and find the Young winner in it by counting the number of voter removals needed to make each alternative the Condorcet winner. Suppose further that we find that candidate *x* is associated with a minimum number, say *k*, of voter removals and is thus the Young winner. Now suppose that we remove a voter who has placed *x* at the bottom of his/her ranking. Let us denote the resulting profile by P'. If for any such P' profile Young's method results in a winner other than *x*, then we must conclude that Young's method is vulnerable to the P-BOT paradox. So let us suppose that *y* is elected by Young's method in P', i.e., that the P-BOT paradox occurs. This means that *y* needed the minimal number of voter removals, say *s*, to become the Condorcet winner. This number, *s*, must be strictly less than $k - 1$ since in P' alternative *x* would need this number ($k - 1$) of removals to become the Condorcet winner. The fact that $s < k - 1$ implies that in P alternative *y* would have needed $s + 1$ removals to become the Condorcet winner. This is strictly less than *k* which was the number *x* needed in P to become the Condorcet winner. Hence *x* could not be the Young winner in P which contradicts the assumption that s/he was. This contradiction leads to the conclusion that examples demonstrating the vulnerability of Young's procedure to the P-BOT paradox cannot be constructed.

Table 5.1 Summary

Method	Sub-type of participation paradox			
	P-TOP		P-BOT	
	CW	CYC	CW	CYC
Successive elimination	No	Yes	Yes	Yes
Bucklin	Yes	Yes	Yes	Yes
Majority judgment	Yes	Yes	Yes	Yes
Black	No	Yes	Yes	No
Copeland	No	Yes	Yes	Yes
Kemeny	No	Yes	Yes	Yes
Schwartz	No	Yes	Yes	No
Young	No	Yes	No	No

5.10 Summary and Conclusions

Table 5.1 summarizes the susceptibility of the eight investigated voting procedures in this chapter to the P-TOP and P-BOT paradoxes under variable electorates. 'Yes' means we provided an example, and 'No' means we explained why no such example exists.

Pérez (2001, p. 602) has stated that:

> Although not all Condorcet [consistent] methods suffer from [Positive and Negative SNSP] paradoxes, the … Minmax method (free from Positive and Negative SNSP) and the Young method (free from Negative SNSP) are, as far as I know, the only exceptions among those proposed in the literature.[1]

As can be seen from Table 5.1, the six Condorcet-consistent voting procedures that we studied are consistent with Pérez's statement.

In the comparative study of voting systems, the monotonicity criterion has been applied widely, and many scholars deem it a necessary property of any reasonable voting system. Our analysis suggests important differences among monotonic systems with regard to properties that relate to the very meaningfulness of participating in elections. Especially, the P-BOT paradox suggests that in quite a few monotonic systems new voters entering the fray may find that by signaling their true preferences on their ballots they may actually help their worst-regarded candidate to win when, without their participation, this candidate would not have won. This may constitute a deterrent for some voters and provide an incentive to abstain from voting. The same is obviously true of systems vulnerable to P-TOP paradox.

[1]This statement is inaccurate. As shown in Chap. 4, two of the well-known Condorcet-consistent procedures (Dodgson's and Nanson's), are vulnerable to the P-TOP paradox but not also to the P-BOT paradox.

References

Felsenthal, D. S., & Machover, M. (2008). The majority judgement voting procedure: A critical evaluation. *Homo Oeconomicus, 25,* 319–333.

Felsenthal, D. S., & Nurmi, H. (2016). Two types of participation failure under nine voting methods in variable electorates. *Public Choice, 168*(1), 115–135.

Felsenthal, D. S., & Tideman, N. (2013). Varieties of failure of monotonicity and participation under five voting methods. *Theory and Decision, 75,* 59–77.

Fishburn, P. C. (1977). Condorcet social choice functions. *SIAM Journal of Applied Mathematics, 33,* 469–489.

Moulin, H. (1988). Condorcet's principle implies the no-show paradox. *Journal of Economic Theory, 45,* 53–64.

Pérez, J. (2001). The strong no show paradoxes are common flaw in Condorcet voting correspondences. *Social Choice and Welfare, 18,* 601–616.

Richelson, J. T. (1978). A comparative analysis of social choice functions III. *Behavioral Science, 23,* 169–176.

Chapter 6
Practical Significance and Open Problems

Abstract The common reaction to social choice anomalies is that while these may be theoretically feasible, their role in practice is likely to be very limited since the profiles giving rise to the paradoxes are exceptional rather than common. We argue that while the significance and observation of the general no-show paradoxes and monotonicity failures may be limited, the same is not true of P-TOP and P-BOT paradoxes. These pertain to the voters' best and worst alternatives. Hence, the occurrences associated with them are most likely to be observed and talked about. Vulnerability to these paradoxes creates bizarre incentives for voters. Failures on monotonicity, on the other hand, have more to do with the legitimacy of the voting outcomes. It is important to find out the structural properties of settings giving rise to monotonicity-related paradoxes. Thus far very little is known about these properties. We have related the paradoxes to the existence of majority cycles in the electorate. Our general finding is that the presence of a core or Condorcet winner does not, in general, make it harder to construct profiles that lead to paradoxes. Sometimes the opposite is true: the presence of cycles makes it harder, not easier, to construct paradoxical profiles. Finally, we speculate about reasons for continued use of non-monotonic rules.

Keywords Voter incentives · Legitimacy of voting outcomes · Majority cycles · P-TOP paradox · P-BOT paradox · Non-monotonicity

Monotonicity-related properties of voting rules are quite central in the overall assessments of those rules. The principle of going to the people makes no sense if by acting in accordance with their preferences the voters are actually harming their own cause. In a sense rules that violate the monotonicity properties discussed above create self-contradictory incentives for the voters. If abstaining from voting may lead to a better outcome (from the voter's point of view), is it reasonable to expect people to exercise their right to vote? The same question pertains to rules which allow for the winners to be turned into non-winners when their support is increased.

This chapter is partly based on Felsenthal and Tideman (2013, 2014).

D.S. Felsenthal and H. Nurmi, *Monotonicity Failures Afflicting Procedures for Electing a Single Candidate*, SpringerBriefs in Economics,
DOI 10.1007/978-3-319-51061-3_6

The former point relates to variable and the latter to fixed electorates. At the same time the former pertains to voter incentives, while the latter to the legitimacy of voting outcomes. A common feature in both is the counterintuitive reaction of the outcomes to certain types of changes in the expressed voter opinions.

A common counter to these kinds of doubts is that, while possible, the situations leading to such bizarre outcomes are so infrequent as to make them insignificant for all practical purposes. And indeed, finding examples demonstrating the incompatibility of the voting outcomes and certain social choice desiderata can be exceedingly difficult for some voting rules, but relatively easy for others. The computational difficulty involved in establishing an incompatibility between a rule and a desideratum, should one exist, does not necessarily reflect the empirical infrequency of the corresponding paradox, but intuitively one would expect that the more difficult it is to envision preference distributions where a voting rule leads to a violation of a plausible criterion, the less likely it is that such violations occur in practice. Yet, the most certain way to exclude criterion violations is to adopt systems that are—not just practically but also theoretically—invulnerable to them.

Our primary focus in this book is on monotonicity violations in variable electorates. These take various degrees of severity. In its standard form the no-show paradox occurs whenever a group of voters with identical preferences is better off by not voting at all than by voting according to its preferences. The difference between outcomes may be associated with any pair of alternatives to be voted upon, assuming of course that the outcome resulting from not voting is preferable to the other outcome. In practice this might render many instances of the no-show paradox pretty insignificant. If the alternative ranked 6-th in a voter's ranking wins, but the 5-th ranked alternative would have won had s/he and his/her associates of like-minded voters abstained, this may not be a cause of concern to the voters. In fact, this would typically not be even known as the voters are often not asked to reveal their entire preference rankings. Of course, each voter can still have one, but typically would not know how many identically minded others there are in the electorate.

In the more dramatic types of no-show paradoxes—the P-TOP and P-BOT ones —the issues of legitimacy of outcomes and questionable voter incentives are far more obvious. It is easy to verify whether one's favorite candidate lost because you and your associates voted according to your true preferences (P-TOP paradox) or your least favored candidate won because you voted against him/her (P-BOT paradox). Hence, arguably the instances of P-TOP and P-BOT paradox are not only more dramatic than the ordinary no show paradoxes, but also more easily detectable. The mere possibility of these paradoxes may be enough to make some voters unwilling to participate in an election. In any event, the possibility is likely to undermine the politicians' calls for active participation of the electorate.

The vulnerability of a voting procedure to some paradox is one thing, but knowing the factors or circumstances that make the paradoxical occurrences more likely would be helpful in explaining their emergence and in seeking ways of avoiding them. The existing literature on monotonicity-related paradoxes in variable electorates has produced relatively scant information about the circumstances prompting them. The proofs that Moulin (1988) and Pérez (1995, 2001) present are not very useful in outlining the general conditions of paradoxes. The auxiliary lemmas used in them provide sufficient, but not necessary conditions for paradoxes. In the preceding we have looked at the P-BOT and P-TOP paradoxes from the point of view of majority cycles in the original preference profiles. It turns out that the presence or absence of cycles can make a significant difference in the likelihood of paradoxes. In some cases—especially in Schwartz's rule—the construction of instances of paradoxes is more difficult in the presence of cycles than in their absence. This may seem counterintuitive since one would expect that in the presence of a Condorcet winner in the original profile the Condorcet extension rules would be quite invulnerable against new entrants placing some other alternative at the bottom of their rankings. But, as is often the case in social choice theory, the intuition is not a reliable guide in characterizing the rules.

The circumstances that make P-BOT and P-TOP paradoxes more likely to emerge, given that the rule under study is vulnerable to them, are still largely unexplored. Besides the cyclicity or non-cyclicity of the initial profiles, no other features of the profiles have been subjected to a systematic study. From the examples shown above and in the literature more generally, one is led to conjecture that in the absence of cycles the initial distribution of support for the 2–3 strongest candidates has to be pretty equal for a paradox to occur. But this is just a conjecture. Should this conjecture turn out to be accurate, the voters would be faced with a real quandary: whether to vote or not to vote when your vote can really make a difference, but at the same time your vote may be maximally damaging to your own interests.

Although all proposed single-winner voting methods involving three or more candidates suffer from some defect, it is generally agreed among social choice theorists that a voting method that is susceptible to non-monotonicity suffers from a particularly serious defect. So why are some of these methods, e.g., Plurality with Runoff or Successive Elimination, or Alternative Vote, actually used? The answer is probably that, if instances of non-monotonicity arise in actual elections, voters or analysts would generally not know that the outcome of the election exemplified some type of non-monotonicity or a closely related paradox, because they would generally not have access to all voters' ballots (and hence would not be able to verify how all other voters ranked the competing candidates).[1] We therefore wonder whether, for example, there would have been a public outcry in France to abolish the Plurality with Runoff voting method in electing its president if, following a runoff of a particular election, it would have been reliably ascertained that, *ceteris*

[1]Potthoff (2011) suggests in a recent article how to construct public opinion polls which may identify the Condorcet winner, if one exists, and thus enable some voters who would not otherwise vote (strategically) for the Condorcet winner to do so and thereby obtain an outcome they prefer.

paribus, presidential candidate x would have been elected if *fewer* voters had voted for x in the first round.[2]

In any case, it would be interesting to verify in future research the a posteriori likelihood of the various types of non-monotonicity and closely related paradoxes occurring under the investigated methods, either by gaining access to the ballots cast in actual elections conducted under one or more of these methods, or by means of suitable simulations. Until such research is conducted we hope that the research reported in this volume will contribute to improved evaluations of the relative merits of the relatively many voting methods that suffer from various types of non-monotonicity and/or from related paradoxes.

References

Felsenthal, D. S., & Tideman, N. (2013). Varieties of failure of monotonicity and participation under five voting methods. *Theory and Decision, 75,* 59–77.

Felsenthal, D. S., & Tideman, N. (2014). Interacting double monotonicity failure with direction of impact under five voting methods. *Mathematical Social Sciences, 67,* 57–66.

Gierzynski, A., Hamilton, W., & Smith, W. (2009). Burlington Vermont 2009 IRV mayor election: Thwarted-majority, non-monotonicity & other failures (oops). *Range Voting Organization.* Accessed October 10, 2016, from http://rangevoting.org/Burlington.html

Moulin, H. (1988). Condorcet's principle implies the no-show paradox. *Journal of Economic Theory, 45,* 53–64.

Pérez, J. (1995). Incidence of no show paradoxes in Condorcet choice functions. *Investigaciones Economicas, XIX*(1), 139–154.

Pérez, J. (2001). The strong no show paradoxes are common flaw in Condorcet voting correspondences. *Social Choice and Welfare, 18,* 601–616.

Potthoff, R. F. (2011). Condorcet polling. *Public Choice, 148,* 67–86.

Smith, W.D. (2007). The Irish 1990 presidential election, won by Mary Robinson: "Success" or "failure" for instant runoff voting (ITV)? *Range Voting Organization.* Accessed October 10, 2016, from http://rangevoting.org/Ireland1990.html

[2]A display of non-monotonicity under the Alternative Vote method has actually occurred and reported recently in the March 2009 mayoral election in Burlington, Vermont. Among the three biggest vote getters, the Republican got the most first-place votes, the Democrat the fewest, and the Progressive won after the Democrat was eliminated. Yet if many of those who ranked the Republican first had ranked the Progressive first, the Republican would have been eliminated and the Progressive would have lost to the Democrat. In March 2010, Burlington replaced the Alternative Vote for electing its mayor with the Plurality with Runoff method—which is also susceptible to non-monotonicity. See the detailed report on this election in Gierzynski et al. (2009). Smith (2007) analyses the Irish 1990 presidential election which was conducted under the Alternative Vote method and concludes (p. 3) that 'it seems clearest to regard this election as suffering from a hybrid form of non-monotonicity (type II) and no-show' paradoxes.

FSC
www.fsc.org
MIX
Papier | Fördert gute Waldnutzung
FSC® C083411

Kolibri 360 GmbH
Ferdinand-Jühlke-Straße 7
99095 Erfurt, Deutschland
produktsicherheit@kolibri360.de